DUBROVNIK TRAVEL GUIDE

ETHAN JONES

©All rights reserved, 2024 ETAN JONES

All content within this book, including images, and any accompanying materials, is protected by
copyright law. The author holds all rights to the
content presented herein. No part of this book may be reproduced, distributed, or transmitted in any form or by any means, electronic or mechanical, including photocopying, recording, or any other information storage and retrieval system, without prior written permission from the author.

TABEL OF CONTENT

INTRODUCTION 11

THE GREAT HISTORY OF DUBROVNIK 11
ANCIENT ORIGINS AND DUBROVNIK'S STRATEGIC SIGNIFICANCE............ 11
DUBROVNIK AND THE RISE OF COMMERCE 13
AUSTRIAN AND OTTOMAN INFLUENCE ON DUBROVNIK........................ 14
MODERN DUBROVNIK: FROM EMPIRE TO INDEPENDENCE..................... 16
BIRTH OF MODERN ART AND THOUGHT IN DUBROVNIK........................ 19
MODERN DUBROVNIK... 21
REVOLUTION AND E-GOVERNMENT IN DUBROVNIK: A NEW ERA OF DIGITAL GOVERNANCE... 24
SUSTAINABLE URBAN LIVING IN DUBROVNIK: A GREEN FUTURE FOR A HISTORIC CITY 27
DUBROVNIK: A CITY OF ART AND CULTURE.. 30

CHAPTER1... 34

PLANNING YOUR TRIP TO DUBROVNIK 34
BEST TIME TO VISIT DUBROVNIK.. 35
VISA AND ENTRY REQUIREMENTS.. 36
TRAVEL INSURANCE 37
BOOKING FLIGHTS TO DUBROVNIK 38
BUDGETING FOR YOUR TRIP TO DUBROVNIK 40
PACKING ESSENTIALS FOR DUBROVNIK... 41
HEALTH AND SAFETY TIPS 42

CHAPTER 2 43

GETTING AROUND DUBROVNIK 43
PUBLIC TRANSPORTATION IN DUBROVNIK 43
RENTING A CAR IN DUBROVNIK 44
CYCLING IN DUBROVNIK 45
TAXIS AND RIDESHARES IN DUBROVNIK 46
NAVIGATING BY BUS 47

CHAPTER 3 49

WHERE TO STAY IN DUBROVNIK 49
LUXURY HOTELS IN DUBROVNIK 49
BOUTIQUE HOTELS AND DISTINCTIVE STAYS 54
BUDGET-FRIENDLY ACCOMMODATIONS 57
VACATION RENTALS AND APARTMENTS 58
FAMILY-FRIENDLY ACCOMMODATIONS 59
BEST NEIGHBORHOODS TO STAY IN 60

CHAPTER 4 62

TOP ATTRACTIONS IN DUBROVNIK 62
DUBROVNIK'S OLD TOWN (STARI GRAD) 63
THE FORTRESSES OF DUBROVNIK 65
LOKRUM ISLAND 66
THE ADRIATIC COAST AND PAST 67
CULTURAL HIGHLIGHTS 68
BEACHES AND THE ADRIATIC SEA 69

CHAPTER 5 71

CULTURAL ENCOUNTERS IN DUBROVNIK 71
DUBROVNIK'S MEDIEVAL LEGACY 71
ART AND ARCHITECTURE IN DUBROVNIK 73
DUBROVNIK'S ROLE IN EUROPEAN HISTORY 75
TRADITIONAL FESTIVALS AND CULTURAL EVENTS 76

CHAPTER 6 78

OUTDOOR ACTIVITIES IN DUBROVNIK 78
EXPLORING THE ADRIATIC COAST AND DUBROVNIK'S SCENIC BEACHES 78
HIKING IN THE KONAVLE REGION 79
BIKING AROUND DUBROVNIK 80
WATER SPORTS AND OUTDOOR ACTIVITIES AROUND DUBROVNIK 81
OUTDOOR EXPLORATIONS IN THE DINARIC ALPS AND BIOKOVO NATURE PARK 82
DAY TRIPS TO THE ISLANDS OF MLJET AND KORČULA 83

CHAPTER 7 84

FOOD AND DRINKS IN DUBROVNIK 84
TRADITIONAL DALMATIAN DISHES 84
BEST RESTAURANTS IN DUBROVNIK 90
STREET FOOD AND LOCAL MARKETS 94
CAFÉS AND PASTRY SHOPS 95
DUBROVNIK'S CRAFT BREWERIES AND WINE 95
MUST-TRY DESSERTS 96

CHAPTER 8 98

SHOPPING IN DUBROVNIK 98
HISTORIC SHOPPING STREETS AND DISTRICTS 98
LOCAL ARTISAN SHOPS AND BOUTIQUES 100
SOUVENIRS AND HANDICRAFTS 102
DUBROVNIK'S MARKETS AND SEASONAL FAIRS 103
ANTIQUE STORES AND VINTAGE FINDS 104
SHOPPING MALLS AND MODERN BOUTIQUES 105
TAX-FREE SHOPPING TIPS 105

CHAPTER 9 107

DAY TRIPS AND EXCURSIONS FROM DUBROVNIK 107
LOKRUM ISLAND – A TRANQUIL ESCAPE 109
DAY TRIP TO KORČULA – CROATIA'S ISLAND GEM 110
STON AND THE GREAT WALLS 112
MONTENEGRO AND THE BAY OF KOTOR 113
MLJET NATIONAL PARK – CROATIA'S GREEN PARADISE 115

CHAPTER10 117

NIGHTLIFE AND ENTERTAINMENT IN DUBROVNIK 117
CLASSICAL MUSIC AND ELEGANT PERFORMANCES 117
BEACH BARS, LOUNGES, AND SEASIDE VIBES 119
TRENDY BARS AND NIGHTLIFE HOTSPOTS 120
LATE-NIGHT CAFES AND COCKTAILS 121
SEASONAL EVENTS AND NIGHT MARKETS 122

CHAPTER 11 .... **123**

PRACTICAL INFORMATION FOR TRAVELERS TO DUBROVNIK **123**
CURRENCY AND EXCHANGE TIPS 123
EMERGENCY CONTACTS AND HEALTH SERVICES 125
TRAVELING WITH CHILDREN 126
ECO-FRIENDLY ACCOMMODATION 128

CONCLUSION **130**

LANGUAGE AND COMMUNICATION **132**

THANK YOU **139**

Map Of Dubrovnik

SCAN THE QR CODE

1. Open your device's camera app.
2. Position the QR code within the camera frame.
3. Wait for your device to recognize the QR code.
4. Follow any prompts that appear.
5. Take action based on the scanned content.

INTRODUCTION
THE GREAT HISTORY OF DUBROVNIK

Ancient Origins and Dubrovnik's Strategic Significance

Dubrovnik's ancient roots stretch back over a millennium, its rich history deeply intertwined with the cultural and maritime legacy of the Adriatic. Long before it became one of the Mediterranean's most celebrated cities, Dubrovnik's location along the Dalmatian coast made it a crucial hub for maritime trade, attracting settlers and sailors from various parts of Europe and past. Initially founded as a refuge by Greek and Roman settlers, the city's strategic position on the Adriatic Sea soon drew the attention of major powers seeking control over its vital trading routes, connecting the Mediterranean to the Balkans and Central Europe.

The recorded history of Dubrovnik begins in the 7th century when the city, then known as Ragusa, was established by refugees fleeing the Slavic invasions. Its favorable location, located between the mountains and the sea, allowed it to flourish as a maritime power. Over time, Dubrovnik developed a reputation as a diplomatic and economic hub, known for its skilled sailors, traders, and astute political leadership. The city's natural harbor became a vital point for commerce, with ships from all over the Mediterranean anchoring to trade goods like salt, spices, and precious textiles. *

Dubrovnik's rise to prominence continued in the Middle Ages, when it became a free city-state under the protection of the Byzantine Empire and later the Republic of Venice. The city's independence, however, was solidified in the 14th century when Dubrovnik, through strategic alliances and diplomatic savvy, secured its status as a republic. This period marked the golden age of the Republic of Ragusa, which became a powerful maritime state, rivaling Venice in its naval and trading prowess. The city's merchants established trade routes with powerful cities like Venice, Constantinople, and past, fueling Dubrovnik's economic prosperity.

The architectural splendor of this era can still be seen in Dubrovnik's UNESCO-listed Old Town, where towering gothic, baroque, and renaissance structures line its marble streets. The famous city walls, constructed during this period to defend against potential invaders, remain an iconic symbol of Dubrovnik's strength and strategic importance. The fortress-like atmosphere of Dubrovnik, coupled with its beautiful blend of cultures, reflects the city's long history of navigating complex political waters while maintaining a thriving, independent spirit.

From its ancient beginnings as a vital maritime trading post to its rise as a powerful city-state, Dubrovnik's legacy as a beacon of commerce, diplomacy, and culture endures today, with each era leaving an indelible mark on its stunning landscape and seafaring spirit.

Dubrovnik and the Rise of Commerce

In the medieval era, Dubrovnik's fortunes soared, establishing the city as one of the most important centers of trade, culture, and craftsmanship along the Adriatic coast. By the 14th century, Dubrovnik, then known as the Republic of Ragusa, had emerged as a significant maritime power, attracting merchants and artisans from across Europe and the Mediterranean. Positioned strategically on key trade routes linking the East to the West, Dubrovnik became a bustling melting pot of cultures. Venetian, Ottoman, and Italian traders mingled with Ragusan merchants, exchanging goods, languages, and ideas that fueled the city's rapid growth. This dynamic period left behind a rich legacy, seen today in the city's grand palaces, churches, and the formidable city walls that continue to stand as symbols of Dubrovnik's medieval prosperity.

One of the most iconic landmarks of this era is the Rector's Palace, a stunning Gothic-Renaissance structure that housed the seat of the Ragusan government. This elegant building not only reflects Dubrovnik's architectural ambition but also its importance as a political, cultural, and economic hub. Just steps away, the bustling Stradun (Placa), Dubrovnik's main street, was lined with merchant stalls and workshops, serving as the heart of the city's thriving marketplace. The square became a gathering place for merchants from all over Europe, where textiles, spices, and precious goods were traded, solidifying Dubrovnik's reputation as a key player in Mediterranean commerce.

During this golden age, Dubrovnik also cemented its role within the broader European and Mediterranean trade networks by aligning itself with powerful maritime republics like Venice and later the Ottoman Empire. Despite maintaining its independence, Dubrovnik's diplomatic relations with these major powers allowed it to expand its reach and influence, ensuring its place as a vital conduit for trade between East and West. The city's merchant fleet became one of the most formidable in the Mediterranean, with Ragusan ships sailing to ports as far as Constantinople and Alexandria. This period of prosperity brought wealth and prestige to the city, fostering cultural and economic growth that continued well into the Renaissance.

Even through political upheavals and changing leadership, Dubrovnik's status as a commercial powerhouse remained secure. The architectural treasures from this golden age, such as the Sponza Palace, the Franciscan Monastery, and the magnificent city fortifications, stand as enduring reminders of Dubrovnik's remarkable rise during the medieval era. Today, these historical landmarks continue to define the character of the city, inviting visitors to stroll through the same streets where medieval merchants once bartered and the rulers of Ragusa shaped the future of this proud maritime republic.

Austrian and Ottoman Influence on Dubrovnik

By the 16th century, Dubrovnik, as the Republic of Ragusa, found itself at the crossroads of major European and Mediterranean powers, including the Ottoman Empire and later the Austrian Empire. Although Dubrovnik maintained its independence for much of this period, its strategic position along key trade routes made it a target of geopolitical interest. The city skillfully guides through these shifting political dynamics, leveraging diplomacy to preserve its autonomy while fostering relations with powerful neighbors.

The Ottoman Empire, in particular, played a crucial role in shaping Dubrovnik's political and economic fortunes. By entering into a tributary relationship with the Ottomans, Dubrovnik secured its safety from Venetian aggression and gained favorable trade privileges throughout the vast Ottoman territories. This arrangement allowed the Republic to continue flourishing as a maritime and commercial hub while remaining largely untouched by the conflicts that ravaged other parts of Europe. Ottoman influence in Dubrovnik is subtle yet notable, particularly in the city's diplomatic approach and trade practices, which enabled it to remain a neutral player amid the region's power struggles.

In the 18th century, Dubrovnik, like much of the Balkans, came under the influence of the Austrian Empire following the decline of the Ottoman presence in Europe. The city's strategic location and resilient economy made it an attractive prospect for the Austrians, who eventually annexed the Republic in 1808 during the Napoleonic Wars. Under Austrian rule, Dubrovnik encountered significant changes in its governance and infrastructure. The Austrians introduced administrative reforms, modernized parts of the city, and integrated Dubrovnik into the broader Austro-Hungarian economic system.

Despite foreign control, Dubrovnik remained a bastion of its distinctive cultural identity, continuing to celebrate its maritime heritage and historical legacy. The city's architecture, a blend of

Gothic, Renaissance, and Baroque styles, remained largely intact, even as new neoclassical structures began to appear under Austrian influence. Landmarks such as the Rector's Palace and the Franciscan Monastery stood as enduring symbols of the city's independent spirit, while newer buildings like the Austro-Hungarian fortifications around the city reminded visitors of the shifting tides of power.

Dubrovnik's eventual incorporation into the newly formed Kingdom of Yugoslavia in the early 20th century marked the end of centuries of foreign dominance, yet the architectural and cultural influences of the Ottoman, Austrian, and other European powers remain integral to the city's historical embroidery. Today, visitors to Dubrovnik can explore these diverse layers of history through its distinctive blend of Mediterranean, Eastern, and Central European architectural styles, which continue to define the city's distinctive charm and enduring legacy.

Modern Dubrovnik: From Empire to Independence

The modern history of Dubrovnik is one marked by resilience, transformation, and the eventual reclaiming of its identity after centuries of foreign rule. By the late 19th century, Dubrovnik, like much of the Balkans, was under the control of the Austro-Hungarian Empire, which had absorbed the region following the decline of the Venetian and Ottoman influences. This period saw significant changes to the city, as it became part of a much larger empire that reshaped its governance, economy, and infrastructure.

Under Austro-Hungarian rule, Dubrovnik maintained its position as a vital maritime hub, though its political autonomy as the independent Republic of Ragusa had long since faded. The city became integrated into the empire's broader economic system, with its architecture and urban planning reflecting the Austrian influence. New public buildings, fortifications, and infrastructure projects were undertaken, blending with Dubrovnik's medieval and Renaissance architecture to create a city that reflected both its rich past and its role in a changing Europe.

However, this period of foreign dominance also fueled a growing sense of national consciousness among the people of Dubrovnik. As part of the broader movements for independence across the Balkans, the early 20th century saw the rise of Yugoslav nationalism, with Dubrovnik playing a key role in the cultural and intellectual debates that shaped the region's future. The city's intellectuals, artists, and politicians were instrumental in advocating for independence from imperial rule, seeking to reclaim the region's identity amid the waning influence of the Austro-Hungarian Empire.

Dubrovnik's trip to independence was interrupted by the turbulence of World War I, which led to the collapse of the Austro-Hungarian Empire. Following the war, Dubrovnik became part of the newly formed Kingdom of Yugoslavia in 1918, marking the end of centuries of imperial control. This was a time of both celebration and adjustment, as the city guide throughd its new role within the Yugoslav state. Despite the challenges of the interwar years,

Dubrovnik remained a center of cultural life, preserving its heritage and continuing to attract artists, writers, and thinkers.

The devastation of World War II brought further turmoil to Dubrovnik, as the city and its people endured the occupation and conflict that swept across Yugoslavia. After the war, Dubrovnik became part of the Socialist Federal Republic of Yugoslavia under the leadership of Josip Broz Tito. While the city encountered a period of rebuilding and modernization, its historical character was carefully preserved. Dubrovnik's cultural and historical significance, coupled with its stunning coastal beauty, made it a key destination for tourism, even during the socialist period.

The fall of Yugoslavia in the early 1990s and the subsequent Croatian War of Independence marked another turning point for Dubrovnik. The city, heavily bombarded during the conflict, once again demonstrated its resilience. After Croatia declared independence in 1991, Dubrovnik became a symbol of resistance and recovery. Extensive efforts were made to restore the damage to its UNESCO-listed Old Town, and today, Dubrovnik stands as both a historical treasure and a modern city fully integrated into the independent Croatian state.

In the years since gaining independence, Dubrovnik has flourished as a global cultural and tourist destination, celebrated for its stunning architecture, rich history, and dynamic modern life. Its trip from imperial control to independence mirrors the broader story of Croatia, a nation shaped by its past but looking confidently toward the future. Dubrovnik today is a city where the old and the new coexist harmoniously, a place where the legacy of empire has given way to the spirit of independence and resilience.

Birth of Modern Art and Thought in Dubrovnik

At the turn of the 20th century, Dubrovnik found itself on the verge of a cultural renaissance, transitioning from a historical stronghold to a dynamic center of modern art, literature, and intellectual discourse. This period, marked by the region's shifting political landscape and growing national consciousness, saw Dubrovnik emerge as a beacon of artistic and intellectual thought in the Balkans.

As the Austro-Hungarian Empire began to loosen its grip on the region, a spirit of revival took hold in Dubrovnik. Local artists, writers, and thinkers began to redefine the city's cultural identity, drawing inspiration from its rich history while pushing toward modernism. Much like the Renaissance period when Dubrovnik was a thriving independent republic, this new wave of creativity sought to blend the city's storied past with the progressive ideals of a changing Europe.

At the heart of this cultural revival was Dubrovnik's literary and artistic community, which flourished amid the political shifts of the early 1900s. Influential figures such as Ivo Vojnović, a Dubrovnik-born playwright and poet, became key voices in shaping the city's modern cultural landscape. Vojnović's works, deeply rooted in the themes of Dubrovnik's past, such as its former independence and aristocratic traditions, resonated with the city's intellectual elite. His plays, including the acclaimed *Dubrovnik Trilogy*, captured the tensions between nostalgia for the city's glorious past and the realities of its changing future.

At the same time, the visual arts scene in Dubrovnik began to thrive, with local painters and sculptors drawing on both traditional Dalmatian themes and modern European influences. Artists like Vlaho Bukovac, who spent his early years in Dubrovnik, returned to the city after studying in Paris, bringing with him the techniques of Impressionism. His work infused the local art scene with new energy, and his depictions of the Dalmatian coast, rich with light and color, helped shape a distinctly modern Dubrovnik artistic style.

The influence of the Secessionist movement, which swept through Europe in the early 20th century, also left its mark on Dubrovnik's art and architecture. The city's intellectuals and architects began to experiment with new forms, blending the old Venetian and Renaissance influences with the sleek, modern lines of Art Nouveau. This melding of past and present is evident in the city's public buildings and private residences from this period, which stand as symbols of Dubrovnik's advancing cultural identity.

The birth of modern thought in Dubrovnik was not confined to the arts alone. Intellectuals in the city played a significant role in the broader national movements that swept across the Balkans during this time. Dubrovnik became a center for political debate, where ideas of nationalism, independence, and cultural preservation were hotly discussed. The city's thinkers were instrumental in shaping the vision of a future Yugoslav state, advocating for unity among the South Slavic peoples while striving to maintain Dubrovnik's distinctive identity within this new political reality.

The outbreak of World War I and the eventual dissolution of the Austro-Hungarian Empire brought both challenges and opportunities to Dubrovnik's cultural scene. The post-war period saw the city briefly integrated into the newly formed Kingdom of Yugoslavia, where it continued to be a hub for cultural and intellectual activity. Dubrovnik's festivals, theaters, and literary circles flourished, with the city's artists and intellectuals continuing to explore new ideas while honoring their deep-rooted heritage.

Despite the political turbulence of the 20th century, Dubrovnik's commitment to preserving its cultural identity never wavered. The city's artistic and intellectual legacy, born from this period of transition, continues to influence Dubrovnik today. Festivals like the Dubrovnik Summer Festival, which showcases theater, music, and art, stand as testaments to the enduring spirit of creativity that has shaped the city for generations.

Today, Dubrovnik remains a dynamic center of modern art and thought, where the echoes of its past blend seamlessly with the innovations of the present. Its galleries, theaters, and festivals celebrate both the city's historical grandeur and its ongoing role as a cultural beacon in the region. From the works of early 20th-century visionaries to contemporary creators, Dubrovnik's trip into modernity is a story of artistic evolution, intellectual awakening, and a deep, abiding respect for the traditions that continue to define this extraordinary city.

Modern Dubrovnik

Today, Dubrovnik stands proudly as a city where history and modernity coexist in harmony, blending the charm of its medieval past with the dynamic energy of contemporary life. This coastal gem, with its ancient walls, shimmering Adriatic waters, and

UNESCO World Heritage status, has evolved into one of Europe's most sought-after destinations. However, past its stunning Old Town and centuries-old fortifications, Dubrovnik has embraced the challenges and opportunities of modern times, transforming itself into a dynamic cultural and digital hub while preserving its distinctive heritage.

The revitalization of Dubrovnik in the late 20th century marked a significant turning point in the city's history. Following the devastation of the Croatian War of Independence in the 1990s, Dubrovnik underwent extensive restoration, determined to preserve its architectural beauty while forging a path toward modern development. The city's resilience and commitment to rebuilding were rewarded, as it soon regained its place as a global cultural treasure and a thriving modern city.

Today, Dubrovnik is not only a destination for history lovers and beachgoers but also a center of innovation and cultural expression. Its local economy has diversified, with tourism playing a central role, supported by creative industries, media, and a growing tech sector. The rise of digital nomadism has found a natural home in Dubrovnik, thanks to the city's welcoming environment, excellent connectivity, and balance of work and leisure. The city has made significant strides in adapting to the needs of a global workforce, offering co-working spaces, networking events, and a lifestyle that blends professional ambition with the beauty of its surroundings.

Despite its focus on modernization, Dubrovnik has not lost sight of its artistic roots. The city is a hub for art, music, and theater, attracting creative minds from all over the world. The Dubrovnik Summer Festival, one of the most prestigious cultural events in

Croatia, showcases the city's rich artistic tradition, hosting performances of classical music, theater, and contemporary art against the backdrop of the city's historic sites. The modern art scene, centered around galleries and cultural spaces like the Dubrovnik Art Gallery, continues to thrive, with exhibitions highlighting both local talent and international artists.

Dubrovnik's modern infrastructure and sustainable urban development initiatives reflect its commitment to being a forward-thinking city. Environmental preservation has become a key focus, with efforts to reduce the impact of mass tourism and protect the city's fragile coastal ecosystem. Investments in sustainable transportation, energy-efficient buildings, and green public spaces have helped the city strike a balance between tourism growth and ecological responsibility.

The city's cultural and architectural revival has been complemented by its culinary renaissance. Dubrovnik has seen a rise in modern restaurants and cafes that blend traditional Dalmatian flavors with innovative cuisine, providing locals and visitors alike with diverse dining options. From farm-to-table eateries offering fresh, local ingredients to Michelin-starred fine dining, Dubrovnik's gastronomic scene reflects both its heritage and its embrace of global culinary trends.

In recent years, Dubrovnik's role as a filming location for major international productions, particularly the popular series *Game of Thrones*, has brought the city into the global spotlight. While the influx of media attention has attracted new waves of tourists, Dubrovnik remains mindful of balancing its fame with the need to preserve its identity and the well-being of its residents.

As Dubrovnik continues to grow and evolve, it remains a place where history informs the present, and tradition guides the future. The city's cobbled streets, ancient palaces, and dynamic cultural scene ensure that its timeless beauty endures, while its embrace of innovation and sustainability promises a thriving future for generations to come. Modern Dubrovnik is a city of contrasts and harmony—a place where the past is revered, and the future is embraced with open arms.

Revolution and e-Government in Dubrovnik: A New Era of Digital Governance

Dubrovnik, renowned for its historical beauty and cultural legacy, is now making waves in an entirely different field: digital governance. As one of Croatia's most forward-thinking cities, Dubrovnik has begun on an ambitious transformation, embracing e-Government initiatives that have revolutionized the way residents and visitors interact with the city. This modernization effort represents a significant shift from its past, positioning Dubrovnik as a leader in digital innovation and public service reform.

At the heart of this digital revolution is Dubrovnik's commitment to making city services more accessible, efficient, and transparent. Gone are the days of standing in long queues at city offices or navigating layers of bureaucratic red tape. With the introduction of a comprehensive e-Government platform, citizens can now access vital services at the click of a button. From registering businesses and applying for permits to paying taxes and accessing public records, nearly every aspect of civic life has been streamlined and moved online.

The platform itself is designed with user-friendliness in mind, ensuring that residents of all ages can easily guide through and complete tasks without hassle. Integrated with secure identification systems, such as electronic ID cards and mobile authentication, the e-Government portal guarantees both convenience and safety, allowing users to manage their affairs without worrying about data breaches or complex procedures.

This digital transformation has also extended to how the city operates its internal systems. Dubrovnik's government departments now utilize cloud-based solutions, advanced data analytics, and artificial intelligence to improve decision-making processes and enhance service delivery. This shift has led to quicker response times, more informed policy decisions, and increased overall efficiency in city operations. Municipal leaders and public officials are now able to access real-time data, helping them address issues faster and with greater precision.

One of the standout features of Dubrovnik's e-Government system is its emphasis on citizen participation. Recognizing the importance of engaging the public in governance, the city has launched a range of interactive tools that allow residents to provide feedback, vote on local issues, and participate in virtual town hall meetings. Through these platforms, Dubrovnik's citizens have a more active role in shaping the policies that affect their daily lives. This collaborative approach has not only enhanced transparency but also fostered a greater sense of community involvement in city governance.

Additionally, the city has integrated smart technologies into its public infrastructure, transforming Dubrovnik into a "smart city" in both form and function. Public transportation, waste management, and energy usage are now managed with cutting-edge technology designed to minimize inefficiencies and reduce environmental impact. Smart parking systems, digital traffic monitoring, and sustainable energy solutions are just a few examples of how Dubrovnik is leveraging technology to improve the quality of life for its residents and visitors.

Tourism, a cornerstone of Dubrovnik's economy, has also benefited from the digital overhaul. The e-Government platform includes services bespoke specifically to tourists, from streamlined visa applications to online booking systems for local attractions. With a large portion of the city's tourism economy dependent on international visitors, these innovations have helped Dubrovnik remain competitive in a fast-advancing global market, especially in the era of smart tourism.

Despite the city's technological advancements, Dubrovnik has not forgotten its historic roots. The e-Government system emphasizes the preservation of the city's cultural heritage by offering virtual tours, digital archives, and online platforms for educational resources about Dubrovnik's rich history. This integration of past and future helps ensures that as Dubrovnik moves forward, it continues to honor the traditions and stories that make it one of the most treasured cities in the world.

As Dubrovnik embraces the digital age, the e-Government revolution serves as a model for cities worldwide looking to blend innovation with civic responsibility. By prioritizing accessibility, efficiency, and citizen engagement, Dubrovnik has not only enhanced the daily lives of its residents but also set the stage for continued growth as a modern, tech-savvy city rooted in its historic legacy.

Sustainable Urban Living in Dubrovnik: A Green Future for a Historic City

Dubrovnik, renowned for its ancient walls and historical charm, is now at the forefront of a new movement—sustainable urban living. As cities around the world face the growing challenges of climate change, overpopulation, and environmental degradation, Dubrovnik has embraced innovative solutions to ensure that it remains not only a cultural gem but also a model for green living. The city's commitment to sustainability reflects a balance between preserving its rich heritage and fostering a future where nature and urban life coexist in harmony.

At the core of Dubrovnik's sustainable transformation is its focus on eco-friendly urban planning. The city has implemented a range of initiatives aimed at reducing its carbon footprint while improving the quality of life for its residents. Public transportation has been overhauled, with electric buses and shared mobility options now available to reduce traffic congestion and pollution. In addition, the city has invested in bike-sharing programs and pedestrian-friendly infrastructure, encouraging residents and visitors alike to choose greener, healthier modes of transport.

Green spaces have also become a central part of Dubrovnik's urban landscape. The city has made a concerted effort to create and maintain parks, gardens, and tree-lined streets that not only provide a natural escape from the bustling city but also contribute to improved air quality and biodiversity. These urban green areas are carefully integrated into the historic setting, ensuring that the natural environment enhances, rather than detracts from, the city's architectural beauty. Dubrovnik's commitment to preserving its coastal ecosystems is equally strong, with conservation efforts in place to protect the Adriatic's marine life and water quality.

Energy efficiency is another key aspect of Dubrovnik's sustainable living initiatives. The city has embraced renewable energy sources, such as solar power, to reduce reliance on fossil fuels. Rooftop solar panels have become a common sight across the city, particularly on public buildings and private residences alike. In addition, energy-efficient buildings are being designed and constructed with sustainable materials, helping to reduce energy consumption while maintaining Dubrovnik's signature aesthetic charm.

Water management is a priority as well, particularly given Dubrovnik's coastal location and its reliance on tourism. The city has invested in water-saving technologies and systems, promoting responsible water usage in both public spaces and private households. Rainwater harvesting and greywater recycling initiatives are becoming increasingly common, helping to ensure that Dubrovnik can sustainably manage its water resources even in the face of changing climate patterns.

Waste management has also undergone a significant transformation. Dubrovnik has introduced comprehensive recycling programs, aiming to reduce landfill waste and promote a circular economy. Public awareness campaigns encourage citizens and businesses to participate in these efforts, making waste separation and recycling an everyday part of life. The city has also taken steps to reduce plastic waste, with bans on single-use plastics in public events and incentives for businesses to adopt more sustainable packaging solutions.

Dubrovnik's focus on sustainability is not limited to its infrastructure but extends to its cultural and tourism sectors as well. As one of Croatia's top tourist destinations, Dubrovnik has recognized the importance of promoting responsible tourism that respects both the environment and local communities. The city has implemented strategies to manage the flow of tourists, ensuring that its fragile ecosystems and historical landmarks are not overwhelmed. Initiatives such as sustainable tours, eco-friendly accommodations, and incentives for green practices among local businesses are all part of Dubrovnik's commitment to maintaining its cultural and natural heritage for future generations.

Education plays a crucial role in Dubrovnik's vision for sustainable urban living. The city has developed programs aimed at raising awareness about environmental issues among both residents and visitors. Schools, community centers, and public campaigns all work to promote sustainable practices, from recycling and energy conservation to the importance of biodiversity and marine protection. By fostering a culture of environmental responsibility, Dubrovnik is ensuring that its green initiatives have a lasting impact.

Dubrovnik's efforts toward sustainable urban living offer a glimpse into a future where cities can thrive while respecting the natural world. By integrating eco-friendly practices into every aspect of daily life, the city is paving the way for a greener, more resilient future—one that honors its past while embracing the challenges of tomorrow. As Dubrovnik continues to lead by example, it stands as a beacon of how historic cities can evolve to meet the demands of sustainability, without losing their distinctive character and charm.

Dubrovnik: A City of Art and Culture

Dubrovnik, long admired for its stunning coastal beauty and medieval charm, has also emerged as a thriving hub of art and culture. While its ancient walls and historic landmarks offer a glimpse into a rich past, the city today is alive with creativity, blending tradition with contemporary expressions of art, music, and performance. Dubrovnik's cultural scene has become a defining feature, drawing in visitors who come not only to encounter its natural wonders but also to engage themselves in its dynamic artistic spirit.

At the heart of Dubrovnik's cultural identity is its deep connection to the arts. The city's streets, squares, and fortresses serve as both inspiration and stage for artists of all kinds. Throughout the year, Dubrovnik hosts an array of cultural festivals that transform the city into a living gallery. The most renowned of these is the Dubrovnik Summer Festival, an event that showcases theater, music, opera, and dance against the backdrop of the city's iconic landmarks. From performances in open-air venues to intimate concerts in centuries-old churches, the festival brings together the best of classical and contemporary arts, attracting talent from across the globe.

In addition to its festivals, Dubrovnik's thriving art scene is evident in its many galleries and exhibitions. Local artists, inspired by the city's breathtaking views and historical depth, display their work in galleries tucked away in the winding streets of the Old Town. These exhibitions offer a fascinating mix of traditional Croatian art forms alongside cutting-edge contemporary pieces, reflecting the city's dual role as both a preserver of heritage and a champion of modern creativity.

Music, too, plays a significant role in Dubrovnik's cultural landscape. The city resonates with the sounds of classical music, jazz, and traditional Croatian folk songs, with performances held throughout the year. Whether it's a string quartet performing in a historic palace or a modern jazz ensemble playing at a waterfront venue, Dubrovnik's music scene caters to a wide range of tastes. The city is also home to several prominent orchestras and choirs, adding to its reputation as a center for musical excellence.

Dubrovnik's cultural richness extends to its museums and historical sites, where visitors can explore the city's artistic and intellectual legacy. The Rector's Palace, a symbol of Dubrovnik's political history, now houses a museum showcasing valuable works of art, rare manuscripts, and historical artifacts. The Maritime Museum, set within the walls of Fort St. John, pays homage to Dubrovnik's seafaring past, offering a glimpse into the city's historic role as a key maritime power. These cultural institutions serve as a bridge between Dubrovnik's illustrious past and its present as a modern city with a deep appreciation for its artistic and historical roots.

In recent years, Dubrovnik has also embraced the world of film and television, with the city's picturesque streets and fortresses providing the perfect backdrop for international productions. The city has gained global recognition as a filming location for the hit series *Game of Thrones*, drawing fans and filmmakers alike. This newfound fame has further cemented Dubrovnik's place as a cultural destination, blending visual arts with the storytelling of modern cinema.

Dubrovnik's embrace of art and culture goes past the traditional, with the city actively encouraging contemporary artists and performers to engage with its historical spaces in new and innovative ways. Street performers, open-air art installations, and interactive public art projects bring a modern twist to the city's ancient streets, fostering a dynamic dialogue between the old and the new. This blend of tradition and modernity makes Dubrovnik a city where history is constantly reimagined through the lens of creativity.

From the masterpieces displayed in its galleries to the performances that light up its public spaces, Dubrovnik's cultural scene is as versatile as the city itself. Whether you're strolling through the narrow streets of the Old Town, attending a world-class theater performance, or enjoying a local folk music concert, Dubrovnik offers a truly immersive cultural encounter. This dynamic city continues to be a beacon of artistic expression, where the past informs the present, and where creativity flourishes at every turn.

CHAPTER 1
Planning Your Trip to Dubrovnik

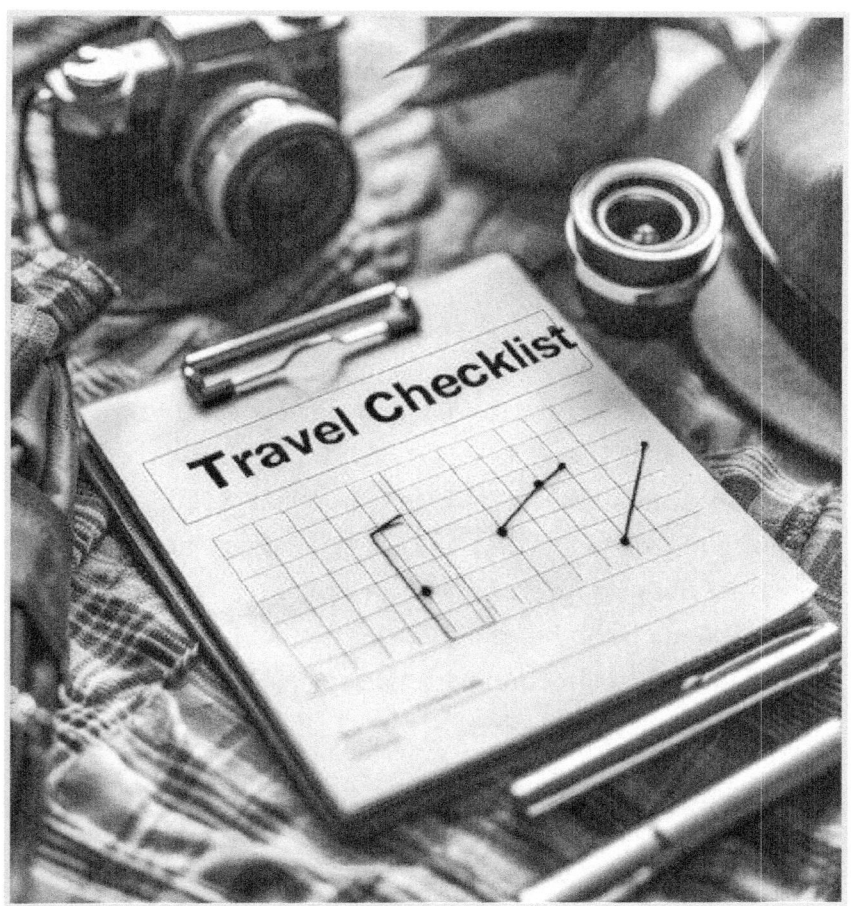

Before embarking on your exploration to Dubrovnik, Croatia's stunning coastal gem, a bit of preparation will ensure you make the most of every corner of this enchanting city. From choosing the best time to visit to understanding entry requirements, booking accommodations, and packing smart, planning ahead will make your encounter smooth and memorable. Let's plunge into the essential elements of organizing your trip to Dubrovnik.

Best Time to Visit Dubrovnik

Dubrovnik is a city that offers a distinctive charm in every season, whether you're drawn to the energy of summer festivals, the calm of autumn, or the magic of winter. The ideal time to visit depends on the type of encounter you're seeking.

1. **Summer (June to August)**:

   Dubrovnik's peak tourist season boasts temperatures between 25°C and 30°C (77°F to 86°F). The city comes alive with events like the famous Dubrovnik Summer Festival, offering open-air theater, music, and art performances. Long, sunny days are perfect for exploring the Old Town and relaxing on the beaches, though expect larger crowds and higher accommodation prices. Booking in advance is a must during this busy period.

2. **Spring (April to May)**:

   Dubrovnik blossoms in spring, with temperatures ranging from 15°C to 20°C (59°F to 68°F), offering comfortable weather for sightseeing. It's an ideal time to explore landmarks like the city walls and Lokrum Island with fewer tourists around. Spring is perfect for a tranquil visit, where you can enjoy the city's beauty at a leisurely pace.

3. **Autumn (September to October)**:

   As the crowds thin and the weather remains pleasant, with temperatures between 15°C and 25°C (59°F to 77°F), autumn is one of the best times to encounter Dubrovnik's cultural attractions and natural surroundings. The fall colors in Gradac Park and along the Adriatic coastline make this season especially magical.

4. **Winter (November to March)**:

   While temperatures in winter can dip to 5°C (41°F), Dubrovnik turns into a quieter, more serene destination. The city's winter festivals, Christmas lights, and festive markets create a cozy atmosphere. Winter is ideal for those who enjoy exploring historical sites without the tourist rush, and it's a great time to find deals on accommodations.

Visa and Entry Requirements

Dubrovnik, like the rest of Croatia, follows the country's entry requirements, and these depend on your nationality.

1. **Visa-Free Countries**:

   Visitors from the European Union (EU), European Economic Area (EEA), and many other countries, such as the United States, Canada, and Australia, do not need a visa for short stays (up to 90 days). A valid passport is required, and your stay must not exceed 90 days within a 180-day period.

2. **Visa Required**:

   For travelers from countries requiring a visa, applying for a short-stay Schengen visa is necessary before arrival. Make sure to provide proof of accommodation, travel insurance, and sufficient financial resources when applying. Always check the latest entry requirements with the Croatian embassy in your country before traveling.

Travel Insurance

While not mandatory for all travelers, travel insurance is highly recommended for peace of mind when visiting Dubrovnik. It can protect you from unexpected incidents, from medical emergencies to trip disruptions.

1. **Medical Coverage**:

   Choose a plan that covers medical emergencies, including evacuation if needed. Dubrovnik's healthcare facilities are excellent, but non-residents without insurance may face high medical costs.

2. **COVID-19 Coverage**:

   In light of the ongoing pandemic, ensure your travel insurance covers COVID-19-related issues, such as treatment and quarantine expenses.

3. **Trip Interruptions**:

   Delayed flights, lost luggage, or unexpected cancellations can be covered under a comprehensive plan, allowing you to enjoy your trip without added stress.

Booking Flights to Dubrovnik

Dubrovnik's international airport, Čilipi (DBV), is located just 20 kilometers (12 miles) from the city center and is well-connected to European cities.

1. **Direct Flights**:

   Many major European cities, such as London, Paris, and Rome, offer direct flights to Dubrovnik, with airlines like Croatia Airlines, British Airways, and EasyJet operating frequent services.

2. **From Outside Europe**:

   If you're traveling from outside Europe, most flights to Dubrovnik will connect through major hubs like Frankfurt, Vienna, or Amsterdam, with seamless connections via carriers like Lufthansa, KLM, and Austrian Airlines.

3. **Budget Airlines**:

   For those traveling within Europe, budget airlines like Ryanair and Wizz Air offer affordable options, particularly if booked in advance.

4. **Booking Tips**:

   Summer and the winter holiday season are peak travel times, so it's wise to book flights 3-6 months in advance to secure the best rates.

Accommodation Options in Dubrovnik

Dubrovnik offers a wide range of accommodations to suit any budget or style, from luxury hotels to charming guesthouses.

1. **Luxury Hotels**:

   For those seeking an indulgent stay, Dubrovnik offers world-class hotels such as Hotel Excelsior and Villa Dubrovnik, both offering breathtaking views of the Adriatic and elite service.

2. **Boutique Hotels**:

   Boutique hotels like The Pucić Palace in the Old Town or Hotel Kazbek offer intimate settings with modern amenities, ideal for those who want to encounter Dubrovnik's distinctive charm.

3. **Budget-Friendly Options**:

   Travelers on a budget will find hostels and affordable guesthouses like City Walls Hostel, offering clean and friendly environments at reasonable prices.

4. **Vacation Rentals**:

For a more personalized stay, vacation rentals through platforms like Airbnb are abundant, particularly in neighborhoods like Lapad or Gruž, providing easy access to both the Old Town and the beach.

Budgeting for Your Trip to Dubrovnik

Dubrovnik, while more expensive than other Croatian cities, can still be a budget-friendly destination with proper planning. Here's a breakdown of typical costs:

1. **Accommodation**:
    - Budget: €40-€60 per night
    - Mid-range: €70-€150 per night
    - Luxury: €200+ per night

2. **Food**:
    - Budget: €7-€15 per meal
    - Mid-range: €20-€40 per meal
    - Luxury: €60+ for fine dining

3. **Transportation**:
   Public buses and taxis are affordable, with a single bus ride costing around €1.50. Dubrovnik's compact nature also makes it easy to explore on foot.

4. **Attractions**:

    Many of Dubrovnik's outdoor attractions, such as walking the city walls, charge admission fees ranging from €10 to €30.

Packing Essentials for Dubrovnik

Dubrovnik's weather varies greatly between seasons, so pack according to the time of year you plan to visit.

1. **Winter (November-March)**:

    Bring warm layers, a heavy jacket, and waterproof shoes, as temperatures can drop to 5°C (41°F) or lower, and rain is frequent.

2. **Spring and Autumn (April-May, September-October)**:

    Light layers and a rain jacket are recommended, as the weather can be unpredictable. Comfortable shoes are essential for exploring Dubrovnik's cobbled streets.

3. **Summer (June-August)**:

    Pack light clothing, sunscreen, and a hat to protect against the strong Mediterranean sun. Comfortable sandals or shoes are ideal for walking.

Health and Safety Tips

Dubrovnik is a generally safe city, but a few precautions can ensure a trouble-free visit.

1. **Emergency Numbers:**

   Dial 112 for any emergency, covering medical, fire, and police services.

2. **Medical Facilities:**

   Dubrovnik has modern healthcare facilities, but if you have any pre-existing medical conditions, bring sufficient medication with you, as not all prescriptions may be readily available.

3. **Travel Safety:**

   Like any tourist destination, be mindful of pickpockets, especially in crowded areas like the Old Town. Stick to well-lit areas at night and use official taxis or ride-sharing services.

By preparing ahead and considering these essential tips, you'll be ready to encounter all that Dubrovnik has to offer, from its rich history to its stunning coastline. It's time to pack your bags and get ready for an unforgettable trip!

CHAPTER 2
Getting Around Dubrovnik

Dubrovnik, with its enchanting blend of ancient architecture and breathtaking coastal scenery, is a city that invites exploration. Whether you're winding through its medieval streets or venturing to its stunning outskirts, Dubrovnik offers a variety of transportation options to suit every traveler's style. From efficient public transportation to scenic cycling routes and car rentals, getting around Dubrovnik is hassle-free and memorable. Here's a guide to help you guide through the city smoothly.

Public Transportation in Dubrovnik

Dubrovnik's public transport system is reliable, affordable, and covers most of the city, including the areas surrounding the Old Town. Buses are the main form of public transportation, making it easy to travel to popular landmarks and scenic spots past the city center.

1. **Ticketing and Payments**: Dubrovnik's bus system uses a straightforward ticketing system:
    - **Single Tickets**: A single ride costs around 15 HRK (€2), valid for 60 minutes from validation. Tickets can be purchased from bus drivers, kiosks, or online.

- Day Passes: For unlimited travel within a 24-hour period, day passes are available for around 30 HRK (€4).
 - Tickets must be validated once on board the bus to avoid fines.
2. **Types of Public Transport**:
    - **Buses**: Operated by Libertas, Dubrovnik's bus system covers both the city center and surrounding areas, including Lapad, Gruž, and past. The buses are frequent and a convenient way to travel to attractions such as the Dubrovnik Cable Car or nearby beaches.
    - **Shuttle Services**: For those traveling to and from Dubrovnik Airport, shuttle buses are available and provide direct transfers to the city center.
3. **Timetable and Frequency**: Buses generally run every 10-15 minutes during peak hours (6 AM to 9 PM). In the evenings, buses run less frequently but still provide access to major areas. Schedules are available via the Libertas app or online.

Renting a Car in Dubrovnik

For those looking to explore past the city, renting a car provides flexibility to visit nearby attractions like the Pelješac Peninsula, the island of Korčula, or the Montenegro border.

1. **Car Rental Companies**: Dubrovnik has a range of car rental companies, including well-known names like Sixt, Avis, and

Hertz, alongside local providers. You can rent a car directly from Dubrovnik Airport or various locations within the city.

2. **Requirements**:
   - A valid driver's license is required, and an International Driving Permit (IDP) is recommended if your license is not in English or Croatian.
   - The minimum age for car rental is typically 21, with some companies applying surcharges for drivers under 25.
   - A credit card is needed for rental security deposits.
3. **Costs**: Rental prices vary but typically range from 200-400 HRK (€25-€50) per day, depending on the car type and rental duration. Be mindful of parking fees and limited spaces, especially in the Old Town.
4. **Parking**: Parking in Dubrovnik's Old Town is limited and costly:
   - **Zone 0**: In the Old Town, parking costs around 40 HRK (€5.50) per hour.
   - **Zone 1 and 2**: In surrounding areas, prices drop to 20-30 HRK (€2.50-€4) per hour. Free parking is available farther from the center.

Cycling in Dubrovnik

Cycling through Dubrovnik offers a scenic and eco-friendly way to encounter the city, especially with the picturesque coastline and parks. While the city's hilly terrain and cobbled streets make cycling within the Old Town challenging, routes outside the historic center are ideal for a leisurely ride.

1. **Bike Rentals**: Several rental services in Dubrovnik offer standard bikes and electric bikes:
   - Prices start at around 100 HRK (€13) per day for regular bikes and 200 HRK (€26) for electric bikes.
2. **Popular Cycling Routes**:
   - **Lapad Peninsula**: Ideal for an easy ride, with coastal paths offering views of the Adriatic Sea.
   - **The ACI Marina Route**: Perfect for a longer, scenic ride along the Dubrovnik River and into the surrounding countryside.
3. **Safety Tips**:
   - Helmets are recommended, though not required.
   - Stick to designated bike lanes and be cautious when cycling on cobblestone streets, particularly in busy pedestrian areas.

Taxis and rideshares in Dubrovnik

Taxis and rideshare services offer convenient, hassle-free transport, especially for those carrying luggage or in need of a quick trip across the city.

1. **Taxis**: Taxis can be hailed on the street or found at designated stands near major attractions like Pile Gate and the main bus station. Fares start at around 30 HRK (€4) with additional charges for distance. It's advisable to use licensed taxis to avoid overcharging.

2. **Rideshare Services**: Uber operates in Dubrovnik, offering a cheaper alternative to traditional taxis. The app allows you to easily book, track, and pay for your ride. A typical ride within the city center costs around 40-80 HRK (€5-€10).
3. **Airport Transfers**: Taxis and Uber provide quick access to Dubrovnik Airport, approximately 20 kilometers from the city center. Expect fares of around 200-300 HRK (€25-€40) depending on traffic and time of day.

Navigating by Bus

Dubrovnik's bus network, operated by Libertas, offers an efficient way to reach various parts of the city and neighboring areas.

1. **Key Bus Lines**:
    - **Line 1A and 1B**: Travel between the Old Town and the Gruž Harbor, where ferries to nearby islands depart.
    - **Line 10**: Connects Dubrovnik with the town of Cavtat, a picturesque coastal destination just 20 kilometers south.
2. **Night Buses**: Night buses operate after regular service hours, ensuring travelers can return to their accommodations safely after a night out in the city.

Tips for Driving in Dubrovnik

Driving in Dubrovnik is straightforward, but some things to keep in mind include narrow streets and busy traffic during peak tourist season.

1. **Road Conditions**: Roads are generally well-maintained, but navigating the narrow streets of the Old Town can be challenging. Traffic jams are common during the summer, especially near major attractions and city gates.
2. **Speed Limits**:
    - Urban areas: 50 km/h (31 mph)
    - Outside urban areas: 80-90 km/h (50-56 mph)
3. **Driving Laws**:
    - Croatia enforces a zero-tolerance policy for drinking and driving.
    - Seat belts are mandatory for all passengers.
    - Headlights must be on at all times, even during the day.

With a variety of transportation options to suit every preference, getting around Dubrovnik is as enjoyable as exploring the city itself. Whether you're using the city's efficient bus system, cycling along the coast, or renting a car to venture past the walls, Dubrovnik makes it easy to uncover all that this stunning destination has to offer.

CHAPTER 3
Where to Stay in Dubrovnik

Dubrovnik, with its enchanting mix of ancient history and Dubrovnik, with its stunning coastal charm and rich historical allure, offers a diverse selection of accommodations to suit every traveler's taste. Whether you're exploring the medieval fortresses of the Old Town or soaking in the Adriatic views from your balcony, Dubrovnik's range of stays ensures that every visitor, whether seeking a luxurious retreat or a budget-friendly base, finds a perfect haven in this enchanting city.

For those longing to encounter the elegance of Dubrovnik's storied past, the city's luxury hotels, particularly in and around the Old Town, transport guests to a world where history meets modern comfort. Envision staying in a beautifully restored palace or a boutique hotel where ancient stone walls meet contemporary style, and your windows open to views of the gleaming Adriatic Sea or the ancient city walls. These accommodations offer more than just a place to sleep—they provide an immersive encounter that connects you to Dubrovnik's cultural heartbeat.

Luxury Hotels in Dubrovnik

If you're in search of world-class service, breathtaking architecture, and prime locations, Dubrovnik's luxury hotels promise an unforgettable stay.

1. Hotel Excelsior

Just a short walk from the Old Town, Hotel Excelsior offers unparalleled luxury with stunning sea views and elegant interiors. This 5-star hotel boasts spacious, modern rooms alongside a lavish spa and private beach access. With its history of hosting celebrities and dignitaries, the hotel blends glamour with comfort, providing an exceptional Dubrovnik encounter.

2. Villa Dubrovnik

For those seeking privacy and sophistication, Villa Dubrovnik is a 5-star retreat perched on the cliffs overlooking the Adriatic. Known for its minimalist design and breathtaking views, this hotel offers luxurious rooms and suites with private terraces. The hotel's fine dining and exclusive beach area add to its allure, making it a top choice for luxury travelers.

3. Hotel Bellevue Dubrovnik

Built into the cliffs, Hotel Bellevue offers a distinctive blend of seclusion and convenience, with its own private beach and stunning views over the bay of Miramare. This 5-star hotel's contemporary design and panoramic windows ensure that the beauty of the Adriatic is always in view. Guests can enjoy an indoor pool, spa, and gourmet dining, all within a short distance of Dubrovnik's Old Town.

4. The Pucić Palace

Located in the heart of Dubrovnik's Old Town, The Pucić Palace is a historic 5-star boutique hotel housed in an 18th-century baroque palace. With just 19 rooms, this intimate hotel provides a luxurious, personalized encounter. The rooms feature elegant furnishings and original artwork, creating a sense of refined opulence.

Boutique Hotels and Distinctive Stays

For those looking for a more intimate and distinctive encounter, Dubrovnik's boutique hotels offer charming accommodations with personalized touches.

1. St. Joseph's Boutique Hotel

Tucked away in the quiet streets of the Old Town, St. Joseph's is a beautifully restored 16th-century property offering luxury suites with a personal touch. Each suite combines modern amenities with period details, making it a perfect choice for travelers who appreciate both history and comfort.

2. Hotel Kazbek

Located on the Lapad Peninsula, Hotel Kazbek is a former 16th-century nobleman's residence turned luxury boutique hotel. This quiet retreat offers spacious rooms with a blend of classic and contemporary decor. The hotel's outdoor pool and tranquil setting provide an escape from the bustle of the city, while still being close to Dubrovnik's main attractions.

3. Villa Orsula

Villa Orsula, set within lush gardens and just a short walk from the Old Town, is an exclusive boutique hotel offering luxury with a Mediterranean touch. Its intimate setting, luxurious interiors, and stunning sea views make it ideal for those seeking a serene and refined stay.

Budget-Friendly Accommodations

Dubrovnik may have a reputation for luxury, but it also offers a range of affordable accommodations that allow travelers to enjoy the city without breaking the bank.

1. Hostel Angelina Old Town

Located within the city walls, Hostel Angelina offers budget travelers a prime location in the heart of the Old Town. With dormitory and private rooms, this hostel provides clean, comfortable accommodations in a historic setting. The friendly atmosphere and helpful staff make it a favorite among backpackers.

2. Guest House Rina

Just outside the Old Town, Guest House Rina offers affordable rooms with stunning views of the sea and city walls. This family-run guest house provides a warm welcome, with simple, clean rooms perfect for budget-conscious travelers who still want to be close to Dubrovnik's main attractions.

3. Dubrovnik Backpackers Club

Located in the peaceful Lapad area, Dubrovnik Backpackers Club offers dormitory and private rooms at reasonable prices. The hostel has a relaxed vibe and is close to beaches, restaurants, and public transportation, making it an ideal base for exploring the city.

Vacation Rentals and Apartments

For those who prefer the flexibility and privacy of a home-away-from-home, Dubrovnik offers a wide range of vacation rentals and apartments, ideal for longer stays or family trips.

1. Airbnb

From chic apartments with sea views to cozy studios in the Old Town, Airbnb offers a variety of options in Dubrovnik. Whether you're traveling solo or with family, these rentals provide the flexibility to cook your own meals and enjoy the city at your own pace.

2. Villa King

Located just outside the city center, Villa King offers modern apartments with spacious balconies and sea views. Each apartment is fully equipped with a kitchen and living area, making it perfect for families or longer stays.

3. Apartments Raic

For those wanting to stay close to the beach, Apartments Raic, located in the Lapad area, offers modern, fully furnished apartments just a short walk from the sea. With its proximity to both the beach and public transport, it's a great option for families or travelers seeking a relaxing stay.

Family-Friendly Accommodations

Dubrovnik is a family-friendly destination with several hotels offering extra amenities to ensure a comfortable stay for guests traveling with children.

1. Valamar Club Dubrovnik

Located on the Babin Kuk Peninsula, Valamar Club Dubrovnik is a popular choice for families, offering spacious rooms, a children's pool, and plenty of activities for kids. The hotel's location, close to beaches and parks, makes it easy for families to enjoy both the city and the natural surroundings.

2. Sun Gardens Dubrovnik

This luxury resort is perfect for families looking for a mix of relaxation and fun. Located just outside the city, Sun Gardens offers family suites, several pools, a kids' club, and a range of activities, from sports to spa treatments. The resort's private beach and family-friendly amenities make it a great option for a Dubrovnik getaway.

Best Neighborhoods to Stay In

Each neighborhood in Dubrovnik offers a different vibe, allowing you to choose the perfect location based on your interests and travel style.

1. Old Town (Stari Grad)

If it's your first time in Dubrovnik or you're a history enthusiast, staying in the Old Town is a must. You'll be steps away from iconic sites like the city walls, Rector's Palace, and Stradun. The Old Town is filled with restaurants, shops, and historic attractions, making it perfect for those who want to be in the heart of the action.

2. Lapad

For a more relaxed atmosphere away from the crowds, Lapad is a great choice. This peninsula offers beautiful beaches, scenic promenades, and plenty of restaurants and cafes. It's ideal for families or travelers looking for a more laid-back vibe while still being close to Dubrovnik's main sights.

3. Ploče

For stunning views of the Old Town and the Adriatic Sea, the Ploče neighborhood is a fantastic option. Many luxury hotels and apartments in this area offer breathtaking vistas, and it's just a short walk to both the beach and the city center.

4. Babin Kuk

If you're seeking a beach escape, Babin Kuk is a quiet peninsula with some of Dubrovnik's best seaside resorts. This area is perfect for those looking to relax by the water while still having easy access to the city's historic sites.

CHAPTER 4
Top Attractions in Dubrovnik

Ah, Dubrovnik! A city that seems to have stepped out of a storybook, with its towering medieval walls, dazzling Adriatic views, and timeless charm. Often referred to as the "Pearl of the Adriatic," this coastal gem enchants visitors with its rich history, dynamic culture, and stunning natural beauty. Dubrovnik is a place where every stone in the ancient streets whispers tales of the past, from medieval battles to maritime glory, offering travelers a magical trip through time and sea.

Whether you're a history buff eager to explore centuries-old fortresses, an exploration ready to kayak the sparkling waters of the Adriatic, or a culture lover looking to encounter world-class festivals, Dubrovnik promises to awaken your sense of wonder at every turn. With the imposing Lovrijenac Fortress and the graceful spires of its churches crowning the skyline, the city perfectly captures the essence of old-world majesty. But beneath the surface, Dubrovnik is a living city, where medieval streets meet contemporary life, filled with art, music, and culinary delights. It's a place where the past dances seamlessly with the present, inviting you to uncover its countless hidden corners.

Dubrovnik's Old Town (Stari Grad)

At the heart of Dubrovnik's allure is its UNESCO-listed Old Town, an impeccably preserved medieval city center encircled by towering stone walls. Every step you take here is like walking through a dynamic history lesson.

1. **Stradun (Placa):** The main thoroughfare of Dubrovnik's Old Town, Stradun, is a marble-paved street lined with baroque buildings that gleam in the sunlight. This central street is

perfect for a leisurely stroll, soaking in the buzz of daily life, with quaint shops, cafes, and historic landmarks at every turn. At one end of Stradun, the Onofrio's Fountain awaits, a masterpiece of medieval engineering, while the bell tower at the other end signals the gateway to Dubrovnik's rich past.

2. **The Walls of Dubrovnik:** Encircling the Old Town, the majestic walls of Dubrovnik offer breathtaking views of the city and the crystal-clear Adriatic Sea. Walking the walls is a must-do encounter, as it takes you past the ancient fortresses and towers, such as Minceta Tower and Fort Bokar, offering panoramic views of the terracotta-roofed city below and the shimmering sea past.
3. **Rector's Palace:** Once the seat of power for the Dubrovnik Republic, the Rector's Palace now houses a museum showcasing the city's illustrious history. With its elegant Gothic-Renaissance architecture, it's a window into the lives of Dubrovnik's ruling elite. Wander through its stately halls, adorned with period furniture, portraits, and relics from the city's golden age.
4. **Dubrovnik Cathedral and Treasury:** Standing proudly at the heart of the Old Town, Dubrovnik's Cathedral is a testament to the city's resilience and faith. The cathedral is famed not only for its baroque beauty but for its treasury, which holds an extraordinary collection of religious relics, including a piece of the True Cross and the golden head of St. Blaise, Dubrovnik's patron saint.

The Fortresses of Dubrovnik

1. **Lovrijenac Fortress:** Perched dramatically on a rocky cliff overlooking the sea, Lovrijenac Fortress is one of Dubrovnik's most iconic structures. Often called "Dubrovnik's Gibraltar," this fortress played a crucial role in defending the city from invaders. Its towering walls and strategic position make it a fantastic spot for history lovers and photographers alike, offering sweeping views of the Adriatic.
2. **Fort Bokar and St. John's Fortress:** These coastal fortresses are key parts of Dubrovnik's formidable defenses. Fort Bokar stands guard at the western end of the city walls, while St. John's Fortress protects the city's maritime entrance. Today, St. John's Fortress also houses a maritime museum, showcasing Dubrovnik's proud naval heritage.

Lokrum Island

Just a short boat ride from Dubrovnik lies the mystical Lokrum Island, a lush escape filled with botanical gardens, hidden coves, and ancient ruins. According to legend, Richard the Lionheart sought refuge here after a shipwreck. Today, it's a peaceful sanctuary where visitors can explore the remains of a Benedictine monastery, wander through tropical plants, and take a dip in the island's secluded bays.

The Adriatic Coast and Past

1. **Srd Hill:** For those seeking the best views of Dubrovnik, a cable car ride or hike up Srd Hill is a must. From the top, you're rewarded with breathtaking vistas of the Old Town's walls, the sparkling Adriatic, and the surrounding islands. There's even a restaurant where you can enjoy a meal with a view that's simply unforgettable.
2. **Elaphiti Islands:** Just off Dubrovnik's coast, the Elaphiti Islands are a dream destination for those seeking tranquility and nature. Each of the islands—Šipan, Lopud, and Koločep—has its own distinctive charm, offering everything from serene beaches to charming villages. Spend the day island-hopping, swimming in secluded bays, and soaking up the Mediterranean sun.

3. **Cavtat:** A picturesque town just a short drive from Dubrovnik, Cavtat offers a quieter but equally beautiful seaside escape. Known for its serene harbor, charming streets, and the Mausoleum of the Račić family, Cavtat is perfect for a peaceful day trip away from the hustle of the city.

Cultural Highlights

1. **Dubrovnik Summer Festival:** If you visit Dubrovnik in the summer, you're in for a treat. The Dubrovnik Summer Festival is an annual celebration of arts and culture, featuring open-air performances of theater, music, and dance against the backdrop of the city's historic landmarks.

There's nothing quite like watching a play or concert within the ancient city walls, under a starry sky.
2. **War Photo Limited:** A distinctive museum dedicated to war photography, War Photo Limited offers a sobering but important perspective on conflicts around the world, including Dubrovnik's own encounter during the Croatian War of Independence. The powerful exhibits remind visitors of the resilience and spirit of Dubrovnik's people.

Beaches and the Adriatic Sea

1. **Banje Beach:** One of Dubrovnik's most famous beaches, Banje Beach offers stunning views of the Old Town and the island of Lokrum. Its crystal-clear waters are perfect for

swimming, and you can relax on the pebble shores while watching boats sail by.
2. **Sveti Jakov Beach:** For a more secluded encounter, head to Sveti Jakov Beach, located just a short distance from the Old Town. Located beneath cliffs, this hidden gem offers spectacular views of Dubrovnik's skyline from the water.

CHAPTER 5
Cultural Encounters in Dubrovnik

Dubrovnik's deep connection to its medieval roots is unmistakable, yet over the centuries, it has evolved into a dynamic city where the echoes of its past harmoniously blend with the pulse of modern life. As Croatia's historic maritime powerhouse, Dubrovnik has long been a crossroads of culture, trade, and ideas, giving the city a distinctive character. From its beautifully preserved medieval walls to its flourishing arts scene, Dubrovnik is a city that celebrates its rich heritage while looking confidently to the future. In this chapter, we dig into the medieval legacy, artistic traditions, and cultural expressions that define Dubrovnik as one of Europe's most enchanting destinations.

Dubrovnik's Medieval Legacy

Dubrovnik's medieval history is central to its identity, and no place captures this better than the Old Town, a UNESCO World Heritage Site and one of the best-preserved medieval centers in the world. Founded in the 7th century, Dubrovnik quickly became a major political, economic, and cultural hub during the Middle Ages. Thanks to its strategic location on the Adriatic Sea, Dubrovnik thrived as a key maritime center, linking East and West through trade routes that brought prosperity and cultural exchange to the city.

1. **Dubrovnik's Role in the Middle Ages:** By the 14th century, Dubrovnik had established itself as a formidable maritime republic, rivaling Venice in its influence and wealth. The city was known for its bustling port, where merchants from across Europe, the Mediterranean, and past exchanged goods ranging from spices and silks to salt, a valuable commodity mined from the nearby salt pans. The wealth generated from this trade is reflected in Dubrovnik's grand architecture, much of which remains intact today.

At the heart of this maritime republic stood Stradun, Dubrovnik's main street, lined with elegant stone buildings and leading to the impressive Pile Gate. This dynamic street was—and remains—the city's commercial and social hub, where the sounds of merchants and craftsmen filled the air. Dubrovnik's strategic importance also made it a center of diplomacy, with its leaders negotiating with empires and kingdoms across Europe to maintain the city's autonomy.

2. **Medieval Architecture:** Dubrovnik's medieval architecture is one of its most defining features. The towering city walls, which encircle the Old Town, stand as a testament to the city's defense against invaders and natural disasters. The walls, complete with towers and bastions, offer breathtaking views of the Adriatic Sea and the red-tiled roofs of the city below.

The Rector's Palace, once the seat of the government of the Republic of Ragusa (as Dubrovnik was known), is a stunning example of Gothic and Renaissance architecture. The palace, now a museum, reflects the wealth and power of Dubrovnik's ruling elite. Another architectural gem is the Franciscan Monastery, which houses one of the world's oldest pharmacies, still in operation today. These structures, along with the numerous churches and public buildings, paint a vivid visualization of Dubrovnik's grandeur during the medieval period.

3. **Life in Medieval Dubrovnik:** Dubrovnik's society during the Middle Ages was marked by a well-defined class structure. The nobility and wealthy merchant families lived in grand stone houses, while artisans and craftsmen formed the backbone of the city's dynamic economy. The city's fortifications and maritime success allowed it to flourish as a center of trade and culture, attracting scholars, artists, and diplomats from across Europe.

Dubrovnik's legal system was also ahead of its time, with the city establishing its own legal codes and diplomatic policies that allowed it to guide through the complex political landscape of the Mediterranean. This commitment to governance and education is still evident today in the city's cultural institutions and schools.

Art and Architecture in Dubrovnik

Dubrovnik's art and architecture reflect the various cultural influences that have shaped the city over the centuries. From its medieval walls and Gothic churches to its Baroque palaces and contemporary art galleries, Dubrovnik's visual landscape is a testament to its rich artistic heritage.

1. **Gothic and Renaissance Influences:** Dubrovnik's Gothic architecture is emblematic of its medieval past, with the Franciscan Monastery and the Dominican Monastery standing as two of the most important examples. The pointed arches, grand cloisters, and complex stonework typical of the Gothic style can be seen throughout the Old Town. The Rector's Palace also features a blend of Gothic and Renaissance elements, showcasing the city's artistic evolution during the Renaissance period.

Stradun and the surrounding streets are home to elegant stone houses with distinctive Renaissance facades, a testament to the city's wealth and its connections with Italian art and architecture during the 15th and 16th centuries.

2. **Baroque Grandeur:** The Baroque era brought a new wave of artistic and architectural splendor to Dubrovnik. After a devastating earthquake in 1667, much of the city was rebuilt in the Baroque style. Churches like St. Blaise's, dedicated to the city's patron saint, are prime examples of Baroque architecture, with their ornate facades, grand altars, and use of light and shadow to create dramatic effects. The Cathedral of the Assumption, another Baroque masterpiece, holds a collection of religious art and relics, further highlighting Dubrovnik's cultural wealth during this period.

3. **Modern and Contemporary Art:** Dubrovnik is also a thriving center for modern and contemporary art. The Dubrovnik Art Gallery, located just outside the city walls,

showcases works by Croatian and international artists, bridging the gap between the city's historical past and its dynamic contemporary art scene. Exhibitions in these spaces often explore the themes of identity, history, and the interplay between tradition and modernity, reflecting Dubrovnik's own evolution as a cultural hub.

Dubrovnik's Role in European History

Dubrovnik has played a significant role in European history, from its time as a powerful maritime republic to its strategic importance during times of conflict.

1. **Dubrovnik as a Maritime Republic:** As an independent city-state, the Republic of Ragusa was one of the most powerful maritime republics in the Mediterranean. Dubrovnik's strategic location and its skilled diplomacy allowed it to maintain independence from larger powers such as Venice and the Ottoman Empire. The city's trade networks spanned from the Balkans to Italy, North Africa, and past, making Dubrovnik a key player in European commerce.

2. **World War II and the Homeland War:** Dubrovnik's history is also marked by its encounters during World War II and the Croatian War of Independence in the 1990s. The city suffered significant damage during both conflicts, particularly during the siege of Dubrovnik in 1991. However, through extensive restoration efforts, Dubrovnik's historical landmarks have been carefully

preserved, and the city has regained its place as a symbol of resilience and cultural pride.

Traditional Festivals and Cultural Events

Dubrovnik is home to a dynamic calendar of traditional festivals and cultural events, many of which have their roots in the city's medieval and maritime past.

1. **Dubrovnik Summer Festival:** One of the most prestigious cultural events in Croatia, the Dubrovnik Summer Festival is an annual celebration of theater, music, and dance. Held in various venues throughout the city, the festival brings together performers from around the world and transforms Dubrovnik into a stage for artistic expression.

2. **Feast of St. Blaise:** Dubrovnik's most beloved religious festival, the Feast of St. Blaise, is held every year in February. The celebration, which dates back to the 10th century, honors the city's patron saint and includes processions, masses, and traditional performances.

77

CHAPTER 6
Outdoor Activities in Dubrovnik

Dubrovnik is not only a city renowned for its historic landmarks and dynamic culture but also a perfect gateway to some of Croatia's most breathtaking natural landscapes and outdoor explorations. From the shimmering Adriatic Sea to the rugged Dinaric Alps, Dubrovnik offers a wide array of activities for nature lovers, explorers, and those seeking to engage themselves in the great outdoors. In this chapter, we'll explore the best outdoor encounters around Dubrovnik, from coastal walks and mountain hikes to kayaking, biking, and scenic day trips that showcase the region's natural beauty.

Exploring the Adriatic Coast and Dubrovnik's Scenic Beaches

A short stroll from Dubrovnik's ancient walls brings you to the sparkling shores of the Adriatic, where sun-kissed beaches and crystal-clear waters beckon. Dubrovnik's coastal beauty offers visitors a range of water sports and scenic spots to relax and enjoy the Mediterranean climate.

1. **Lapad Bay and Sunset Beach:** Lapad Bay is one of the most popular coastal areas in Dubrovnik, with its long

promenade, scenic beach spots, and numerous cafes and restaurants. Sunset Beach, a key highlight of the bay, offers calm waters perfect for swimming and paddleboarding. The beach's soft pebbles and clear waters provide a peaceful retreat, while the surrounding paths are ideal for a leisurely walk or jog along the shoreline.

2. **Banje Beach:** Just steps from the Old Town's eastern gate, Banje Beach offers stunning views of Dubrovnik's city walls and Lokrum Island. This lively beach is great for those seeking water sports, such as jet skiing, parasailing, or kayaking. After a day of sunbathing and swimming, visitors can relax at the beachside bars and restaurants that line the coast.

3. **Lokrum Island:** For a more secluded outdoor encounter, hop on a short boat ride from Dubrovnik to Lokrum Island, a nature reserve located just off the coast. Known for its lush forests, walking trails, and hidden coves, Lokrum is a hiker's paradise. Visitors can swim in the island's saltwater lake, explore the medieval monastery, or enjoy the breathtaking views from the island's highest point, Fort Royal.

Hiking in the Konavle Region

For those looking to explore Dubrovnik's stunning hinterland, the Konavle region offers dramatic landscapes, traditional villages, and diverse hiking opportunities. Located just a short drive south of the city, Konavle's pristine nature and scenic trails are perfect for outdoor enthusiasts.

1. **Hiking Trails in Konavle:** Konavle is home to a variety of well-marked hiking trails, many of which offer stunning views of the surrounding mountains, vineyards, and the Adriatic coastline. One of the most popular routes is the trail to the top of Sniježnica, the highest peak in southern Croatia. At 1,234 meters above sea level, Sniježnica rewards hikers with panoramic views of the Konavle valley, Dubrovnik's coastline, and Montenegro.

2. **Cavtat:** After a day of hiking in the Konavle region, take a break in the charming coastal town of Cavtat, located just south of Dubrovnik. Known for its picturesque harbor, Cavtat offers a peaceful escape with its palm-lined promenades, quiet beaches, and lovely waterfront cafes. Visitors can also explore the town's historical landmarks, such as the Rector's Palace and the Racic Mausoleum.

Biking Around Dubrovnik

With its scenic coastal roads, quiet countryside lanes, and panoramic views, Dubrovnik and its surroundings are ideal for cycling. Whether you're looking for a relaxing ride along the coast or a challenging ascent through the hills, biking is an eco-friendly way to explore the region.

1. **Cycling Along the Dubrovnik Coastline:** One of the best cycling routes in the area follows the coast from Dubrovnik

to the small village of Trsteno, known for its beautiful botanical gardens. The scenic route offers stunning views of the Adriatic Sea, passing through quaint villages and olive groves. Along the way, you can stop for a swim at one of the many secluded beaches or enjoy a picnic with a view.

2. **Exploring the Elaphiti Islands by Bike:** For a more adventurous biking encounter, head to the Elaphiti Islands, a group of islands located northwest of Dubrovnik. The islands of Lopud and Šipan are particularly popular with cyclists, offering quiet roads, olive orchards, and charming villages. Take a ferry from Dubrovnik and rent a bike to explore these peaceful, car-free islands at your own pace.

Water Sports and Outdoor Activities Around Dubrovnik

Dubrovnik's coastal location makes it an ideal destination for water sports and other outdoor activities that allow visitors to embrace the region's natural beauty from a different perspective.

1. **Kayaking Around the City Walls:** One of the most popular outdoor encounters in Dubrovnik is sea kayaking along the city's medieval walls. Guided tours take visitors around the Old Town, offering stunning views of the fortress, Lokrum Island, and hidden beaches that are only accessible by kayak. Whether you choose a sunset paddle or a daytime exploration, kayaking provides a distinctive way to encounter Dubrovnik from the water.

2. **Windsurfing and Paddleboarding:** For water sports enthusiasts, Dubrovnik offers excellent conditions for windsurfing and paddleboarding. The beaches around the Lapad Peninsula and the waters near Dubrovnik's Marina are popular spots for these activities. With steady winds and calm waters, both beginners and encountered surfers can enjoy the thrill of gliding across the Adriatic.

Outdoor Explorations in the Dinaric Alps and Biokovo Nature Park

For those seeking more adventurous encounters, the nearby Dinaric Alps and Biokovo Nature Park provide dramatic landscapes and exciting outdoor activities just a short trip from Dubrovnik.

1. **Hiking in Biokovo Nature Park:** Located north of Dubrovnik, Biokovo Nature Park is a stunning mountain range known for its rugged peaks, limestone cliffs, and diverse flora and fauna. Hiking in Biokovo offers panoramic views of the Adriatic Sea and the islands below, as well as the opportunity to explore hidden caves and historic mountain villages. The park's highest peak, Sveti Jure, is the second-highest mountain in Croatia and provides a challenging yet rewarding climb for encountered hikers.

2. **Mountaineering in the Dinaric Alps:** For more encountered explorations, the Dinaric Alps offer some of the best mountaineering opportunities in the region. The Orjen and Prenj mountain ranges, located just across the border in

Montenegro and Bosnia, feature dramatic landscapes and challenging ascents. With well-marked trails and breathtaking views, these mountain ranges are perfect for those seeking to explore the wilderness past Dubrovnik.

Day Trips to the Islands of Mljet and Korčula

For those looking to venture past Dubrovnik, nearby islands such as Mljet and Korčula offer the perfect day trips filled with nature, history, and relaxation.

1. **Mljet National Park:** A visit to Mljet Island offers the perfect combination of natural beauty and tranquility. The island's national park is home to saltwater lakes, dense forests, and scenic walking trails. Visitors can hike or bike around the lakes, swim in the crystal-clear waters, or explore the island's historic monastery located on a small island within one of the lakes.

2. **Korčula Island:** Korčula, often referred to as the birthplace of the famous explorer Marco Polo, is known for its medieval old town, lush vineyards, and beautiful beaches. A day trip to Korčula allows visitors to explore the island's charming villages, sample local wines, and enjoy the relaxed pace of island life.

CHAPTER 7
Food and Drinks in Dubrovnik

Dubrovnik—a city where every stone whisper tales of ancient civilizations, where winding alleys guide you through stunning squares, and where the Adriatic breeze carries with it the scent of both history and dynamic modern life. But past its historic charm lies another dimension to this enchanting city: its food. Dubrovnik's culinary scene is a delicious blend of rustic traditions, hearty Mediterranean meals, and modern gastronomic creativity, drawing inspiration from Croatia's coastal bounty, fertile land, and centuries of cultural influences. From fresh seafood dishes to traditional Dalmatian specialties, Dubrovnik's food is as enchanting as its past. Ready for a culinary trip? Let's plunge into Dubrovnik's rich food culture.

Traditional Dalmatian Dishes

At the heart of Dubrovnik's culinary identity lies a deep connection to the Adriatic Sea and the region's agricultural roots. The food here reflects the flavors of the Mediterranean—simple, fresh, and full of soul. These traditional Dalmatian dishes have nourished generations and continue to captivate both locals and visitors with their taste and authenticity.

1. **Peka (Meat or Seafood Cooked Under the Bell)**

No culinary trip through Dubrovnik is complete without trying peka, a traditional Dalmatian dish cooked under an iron bell over hot coals. Whether it's slow-cooked lamb, octopus, or veal, the result is a tender, flavorful feast. Vegetables such as potatoes and carrots are cooked alongside the meat or seafood, absorbing all the rich juices. Peka is typically reserved for special occasions and takes several hours to prepare, making it a must-try when dining at local taverns.

2. **Black Risotto (Crni Rižot)**

A true symbol of the Adriatic coast, black risotto is made with cuttlefish or squid, infused with their ink to give the dish its distinctive dark color. The risotto is rich, tasty, and brimming with the taste of the sea. Cooked with onions, garlic, olive oil, and a splash of wine, this dish is often garnished with a bit of parsley and is a staple in Dubrovnik's coastal cuisine. It's a must for seafood lovers seeking a taste of the Adriatic.

3. **Dalmatian Pašticada (Slow-Cooked Beef Stew)**

Pašticada is one of the most beloved traditional dishes of Dalmatia, especially in Dubrovnik. This slow-cooked beef stew is marinated for hours in vinegar, garlic, and wine before being simmered with vegetables and prunes. The result is a deeply flavorful, melt-in-your-mouth dish often served with homemade gnocchi or pasta. Pašticada is a symbol of celebration and comfort, a dish passed down through generations.

4. **Octopus Salad**

Octopus salad is a refreshing and light dish that showcases the fresh seafood Dubrovnik is famous for. The octopus is boiled until tender, then mixed with olive oil, lemon juice, garlic, and parsley, resulting in a dynamic and delicious salad. It's typically served cold as an appetizer and is perfect for a summer day by the sea.

5. **Fritule (Dalmatian Doughnuts)**

These small, fried dough balls are a popular sweet treat across Dalmatia. Flavored with citrus zest, raisins, and a splash of rakija (Croatian brandy), fritule are often dusted with powdered sugar. They're especially popular during the holidays but can be enjoyed year-round at markets and cafés throughout Dubrovnik.

Best Restaurants in Dubrovnik

Dubrovnik's culinary scene is as varied as its history, with everything from fine-dining restaurants offering modern takes on Dalmatian cuisine to cozy konobas (taverns) serving hearty traditional fare. Here are some of the top restaurants in Dubrovnik where you can taste the best of local cuisine.

1. **Nautika**

Located right by the city walls with stunning views of the Adriatic Sea and Fort Lovrijenac, Nautika is one of Dubrovnik's most renowned fine-dining restaurants. Specializing in fresh seafood and Mediterranean dishes, Nautika's menu offers an exquisite encounter with traditional flavors presented in a modern, gourmet style. Signature dishes include lobster from the nearby island of Vis and Adriatic shrimp, all prepared with local ingredients.

2. **Proto**

Known for its fresh seafood and elegant setting, Proto has been a Dubrovnik institution since 1886. Located in the heart of the Old Town, Proto offers a refined dining encounter that highlights the region's maritime traditions. Specialties include octopi's salad, grilled fish, and black risotto. The restaurant's rooftop terrace is the perfect place to enjoy a meal while overlooking the historic streets below.

3. **Taj Mahal**

For a taste of something different in Dubrovnik, Taj Mahal offers a distinctive blend of Bosnian and Dalmatian cuisine. This restaurant specializes in hearty, flavorful dishes like cevapi (grilled minced meat sausages), lamb baked in a clay oven, and delicious burek (tasty pastries filled with meat or cheese). The cozy, warm atmosphere adds to the charm, making it a favorite among locals and visitors alike.

4. **Kopun**

Kopun, located just steps away from the Jesuit Stairs in the Old Town, is known for its traditional Croatian dishes with a focus on authentic, slow-cooked meals. The restaurant's specialty is capon (castrated rooster), a dish with historical roots in Dubrovnik's noble families. It's cooked with honey, lemon, and herbs, creating a distinctive and flavorful encounter.

Street Food and Local Markets

For a more casual and immersive introduction to Dubrovnik's food scene, the city's street food and markets offer a variety of quick, delicious bites that reflect local flavors.

1. **Burek**

A popular street food across the Balkans, burek is a flaky pastry filled with meat, cheese, or spinach. It's perfect for a quick snack while exploring Dubrovnik's Old Town. You'll find burek at bakeries and small eateries, with locals often enjoying it as a breakfast treat or a light lunch.

2. **Dubrovnik Green Market**

Located near Gundulić Square, Dubrovnik's Green Market is the place to encounter the city's fresh produce, homemade cheeses, olive oil, and traditional sweets. The market is filled with stalls selling seasonal fruits and vegetables, as well as locally made honey and jams. It's a great spot to pick up picnic supplies or sample regional delicacies like dried figs and sugared almonds.

3. **Arancini and Bruštulani Migduli**

Arancini (candied orange peel) and bruštulani migduli (candied almonds) are traditional Dalmatian sweets that you'll find at markets and specialty shops throughout Dubrovnik. These sweet, crunchy treats are perfect for snacking while strolling through the city or as a souvenir to take home.

Cafés and Pastry Shops

Dubrovnik's café culture is deeply ingrained in daily life, offering visitors a chance to relax with a coffee and a sweet treat while soaking in the city's atmosphere.

1. **Gradska Kavana Arsenal**

Situated in a prime location overlooking Dubrovnik's Old Port, Gradska Kavana Arsenal is a popular spot for enjoying a coffee or dessert with a view. The café offers a variety of cakes, including the famous Dubrovnik rožata, a local version of crème caramel. With its stunning terrace and historic setting, it's a perfect place to unwind.

2. **Café Buza**

Café Buza is one of Dubrovnik's most distinctive spots, perched on the cliffs just outside the city walls. Known for its spectacular views of the Adriatic, this cliffside bar is the perfect place to sip on a cold drink or enjoy a coffee while watching the sunset. The atmosphere is casual, making it a great spot for a laid-back afternoon.

Dubrovnik's Craft Breweries and Wine

While Dubrovnik is known for its wines—particularly the robust red wines from the Pelješac Peninsula—the city's craft beer scene has been steadily growing. Local breweries offer a range of refreshing ales and lagers, often brewed with local ingredients.

1. **DUB Brewery**

DUB Brewery is Dubrovnik's first craft brewery, offering a selection of locally brewed beers. Their flagship beer, the DUB Pale Ale, is a refreshing choice after a day of sightseeing. You can sample their beers at various bars and restaurants throughout the city, or visit the brewery itself for a tasting.

2. **Malvasija Wine**

Dubrovnik is also known for its local wine, particularly Malvasija, a white wine variety that has been cultivated in the region for centuries. Many restaurants and wine bars in the city offer Malvasija by the glass, allowing you to sample this crisp, aromatic wine alongside your meal.

Must-Try Desserts

Dubrovnik's desserts are a reflection of the region's rich history, blending influences from the Mediterranean, Venice, and past. No visit is complete without sampling some of the city's most beloved sweets.

1. **Rožata**

A Dubrovnik specialty, rožata is a custard-like dessert similar to crème caramel, flavored with rose liqueur. This silky-smooth dessert is typically served chilled and is the perfect way to end a meal. You'll find it on the menu at most traditional restaurants and cafés throughout the city.

2. **Kotonjata**

Kotonjata is a quince jelly dessert, often made during the autumn months when quince is in season. This sweet, firm jelly is usually cut into slices and served as a treat with coffee or after a meal.

CHAPTER 8
Shopping in Dubrovnik

Ah, Dubrovnik—the pearl of the Adriatic, where ancient stone walls rise majestically against the crystal-clear sea and narrow streets lead you through centuries of history. Past its architectural marvels and cultural heritage, Dubrovnik offers a rich shopping encounter that marries the old-world charm of its medieval past with modern flair. Whether you're strolling through the historic alleys of the Old Town in search of distinctive artisanal goods, browsing local markets for handcrafted treasures, or indulging in high-end fashion at modern boutiques, Dubrovnik's shopping scene promises something for every taste.

From bustling squares to hidden shops in the ancient stone alleys, Dubrovnik invites you to uncover its diverse offerings. In this chapter, we'll explore the best places to shop, guide you through Dubrovnik's artisan boutiques, introduce you to local markets, and offer tips for making the most of your shopping encounter in this enchanting coastal city.

Historic Shopping Streets and Districts

Dubrovnik's Old Town, a UNESCO World Heritage Site, is not only a living museum but also a shopper's haven. With its atmospheric streets, charming squares, and centuries-old architecture, the Old Town offers a magical setting for a shopping spree.

1. **Stradun (Placa Street)**

   The heart of Dubrovnik's Old Town, Stradun, is a bustling thoroughfare lined with a variety of shops offering everything from Croatian fashion to locally made jewelry and souvenirs. As you stroll along this wide, marble-paved street, you'll find a mix of high-end boutiques, charming local shops, and cafes where you can take a break from your shopping exploration. Stradun is also home to some of Dubrovnik's most iconic landmarks, making it the perfect place to combine sightseeing with shopping.

2. **Gundulić Square Market**

   Located just off Stradun, Gundulić Square hosts a dynamic daily market where locals sell fresh produce, homemade jams, honey, and lavender products. The market also offers a range of handcrafted souvenirs such as traditional Croatian textiles, ceramics, and olive wood carvings. It's the ideal spot to pick up some authentic Dubrovnik goods and soak in the lively atmosphere of the city's local life.

3. **Peline Street**

   For those interested in discovering Dubrovnik's bohemian side, Peline Street, located just outside the city walls, is a hidden gem filled with independent boutiques, artisan shops, and vintage stores. Here, you'll find one-of-a-kind treasures, from handmade jewelry to retro fashion and quirky souvenirs. It's the perfect street for those looking for something a little different from the typical tourist offerings.

4. **Prijeko Street**

   Prijeko Street, running parallel to Stradun, is a quieter but equally charming street known for its traditional craftsmanship. The small boutiques and galleries along Prijeko specialize in local artisans' work, from complexly designed lace and embroidery to paintings and ceramics. It's the place to find handmade gifts and keepsakes that reflect Dubrovnik's artistic spirit.

Local Artisan Shops and Boutiques

Dubrovnik is home to a talented community of artisans who create beautiful, handcrafted goods that capture the essence of the city's heritage. Whether you're looking for complex lace, distinctive jewelry, or authentic Croatian art, Dubrovnik's artisan shops are brimming with treasures.

1. **Clara Stones Jewelry**

   For lovers of fine jewelry, Clara Stones offers stunning pieces crafted from the region's famous coral. This boutique specializes in red Adriatic coral jewelry, combining traditional craftsmanship with contemporary design. Each piece is hand-made, reflecting the natural beauty of the coral and Dubrovnik's rich maritime tradition. A visit to Clara Stones is not only about shopping; it's an opportunity to learn about the art of coral jewelry-making, with the shop often hosting demonstrations of the complex process.

2. **Dubrovnik House of Marin Držić**

For history enthusiasts, the Dubrovnik House of Marin Držić offers a selection of medieval-inspired souvenirs, art prints, and literature that celebrates Dubrovnik's rich cultural legacy. Marin Držić, one of Croatia's greatest Renaissance playwrights, is honored in this boutique, which offers books, replicas of historical artifacts, and traditional Dubrovnik items. It's a must-visit for those looking to take home a piece of the city's literary and artistic heritage.

3. **Maria Store**

For a high-end shopping encounter, head to Maria Store, Dubrovnik's premier luxury boutique. Located on Stradun, this shop features designer brands from both Croatia and abroad, offering a curated selection of fashion, accessories, and shoes. Maria Store is known for its sophisticated style and is the go-to destination for those seeking the latest in international fashion trends.

4. **Art by Stjepko**

   A distinctive art gallery located within the city walls, Art by Stjepko showcases the work of Croatian artist Stjepko Mamić, known for his colorful, maritime-inspired paintings. His works capture the beauty of the Adriatic Sea, making them perfect souvenirs for art lovers. The gallery offers a range of original paintings and prints, allowing visitors to take a piece of Dubrovnik's seafaring spirit home with them.

Souvenirs and Handicrafts

Dubrovnik is a haven for those seeking authentic souvenirs and handicrafts that tell the story of the city's cultural and historical richness. From traditional lace to handcrafted ceramics, Dubrovnik's shops are filled with items that reflect the region's heritage.

1. **Lace from Konavle**

   Lace-making is an ancient craft in the Dubrovnik region, particularly in the nearby Konavle area, where women have been creating complex lacework for centuries. You'll find beautiful lace tablecloths, doilies, and handkerchiefs in many of Dubrovnik's artisan shops. Each piece is a work of art, making lace one of the most cherished souvenirs from the city.

2. **Olive Wood Products**

The olive tree has long been a symbol of the Mediterranean, and in Dubrovnik, artisans craft beautiful household items from its wood. From olive wood bowls and cutting boards to hand-carved utensils, these products are both functional and decorative. They make for thoughtful gifts that showcase the natural beauty and craftsmanship of the region.

3. **Rakija (Croatian Brandy)**

For those interested in local spirits, rakija is a traditional Croatian brandy made from various fruits, including plums, apricots, and herbs. Many shops in Dubrovnik sell bottles of rakija, often in beautifully decorated glass containers. This strong, flavorful drink is a perfect souvenir to bring a taste of Croatia back home.

Dubrovnik's Markets and Seasonal Fairs

For a truly immersive shopping encounter, Dubrovnik's markets and seasonal fairs offer the chance to mingle with locals while discovering fresh produce, handcrafted goods, and distinctive treasures.

1. **Gundulić Square Market**

Dubrovnik's daily market in Gundulić Square is a dynamic and colorful affair, offering a mix of fresh fruits, vegetables, and local delicacies. Alongside the food stalls, you'll find artisans selling handmade soaps, lavender products, and other traditional Croatian goods. It's the perfect place to pick up some edible souvenirs or gifts infused with the fragrances of the Mediterranean.

2. **Dubrovnik Summer Festival Market**

   During the Dubrovnik Summer Festival, the city comes alive with cultural events, performances, and a special market where local artisans showcase their crafts. The market offers a range of products, from handcrafted jewelry to traditional Croatian costumes and textiles. It's an ideal time to visit Dubrovnik if you're looking for distinctive, festival-exclusive items.

3. **Christmas Market in Dubrovnik**

   The holiday season transforms Dubrovnik into a winter wonderland, with festive lights, decorations, and a Christmas market in Luža Square. The market offers a range of holiday treats, including mulled wine, gingerbread, and local crafts. It's a magical encounter, perfect for finding Christmas gifts while enjoying the festive atmosphere.

Antique Stores and Vintage Finds

For those with a passion for history, Dubrovnik's antique stores offer a fascinating glimpse into the city's past. From vintage books and furniture to relics from Dubrovnik's maritime days, the city's antique shops are treasure troves waiting to be explored.

1. **Dubrovnik Antiques**

   Located just off Stradun, Dubrovnik Antiques is a well-known shop offering a curated selection of antiques, including fine art, furniture, jewelry, and maritime memorabilia. The shop's collection is carefully chosen to reflect Dubrovnik's rich history, making it a perfect stop for those looking to take home a piece of the city's heritage.

Shopping Malls and Modern Boutiques

While Dubrovnik's charm lies in its historic streets and markets, the city also offers modern shopping malls and boutiques that cater to contemporary tastes.

1. **DOC Shopping Center**

   For a more modern shopping encounter, DOC Shopping Center, located just outside the Old Town, offers a range of fashion stores, electronics, and beauty retailers. It's a convenient place to shop for more practical items or international brands.

Tax-Free Shopping Tips

For non-EU residents, shopping in Dubrovnik comes with the added benefit of tax-free shopping, allowing you to reclaim VAT (Value Added Tax) on your purchases.

1. **Eligibility for Tax-Free Shopping**

   To qualify for tax-free shopping, non-EU residents must make a minimum purchase (typically around 740 HRK) at participating stores. Look for the "Tax-Free Shopping" sign or ask the shop staff if they offer tax-free services.

2. **Claiming Your Refund**

   After making your purchase, request a tax-free form from the shop. When you leave Croatia, present this form, along with your goods, to customs at the airport or border crossing to have it stamped. You can then claim your refund at the airport or have it credited to your account.

Whether you're exploring Dubrovnik's historic streets, visiting local markets, or browsing artisan boutiques, the city offers a shopping encounter that is as rich and varied as its cultural heritage. From handcrafted souvenirs to high-end fashion, there's something for every kind of shopper in this beautiful coastal city. Happy shopping!

Happy shopping!

CHAPTER 9
Day Trips and Excursions from Dubrovnik

Ah, Dubrovnik—a city where the shimmering Adriatic meets towering ancient walls, and where centuries of history are etched into every stone. As you wander through its narrow, sun-kissed streets, you can feel the whispers of medieval times, while the dynamic energy of modern life pulses through every corner. Dubrovnik is a place where history and the contemporary world blend seamlessly, where bustling cafes, lively squares, and creative enclaves breathe life into the old city. But past Dubrovnik's enchanting history lies something even more enchanting—an invitation to explore some of the most breathtaking landscapes and cultural treasures that southern Croatia has to offer. From serene island getaways to majestic fortresses, and from lush Mediterranean forests to the sparkling blue waters of the Adriatic, Dubrovnik is the perfect launching point for discovering the natural beauty and rich history of the region.

Dubrovnik's position on the southern Croatian coast makes it an ideal gateway to countless day trips and excursions. Whether you yearn to explore the peaceful villages that dot the Dalmatian countryside, delve into Croatia's rich and often dramatic history, or soak in the sun along pristine beaches, Dubrovnik offers an exploration for every kind of traveler. Past the city's iconic walls, you'll uncover idyllic islands, charming medieval towns, therapeutic natural springs, and rolling hills covered in olive groves and vineyards.

For those captivated by Croatia's cultural embroidery, Dubrovnik's proximity to historical sites such as Ston, with its world-famous walls and salt pans, or the neighboring country of Montenegro, home to the stunning Bay of Kotor, offers deep insights into the region's complex past. Each visit reveals another layer of Croatia's story, providing an opportunity to reflect on its history while basking in the beauty of the present. And with Dubrovnik situated near other regional gems, it's easy to expand your trip into a multi-country exploration, with places like Mostar in Bosnia and Herzegovina or the dynamic cities of Montenegro just a short trip away.

Whether you're dreaming of hiking through pine-covered hills, uncovering the secrets of ancient fortresses, or indulging in the relaxing traditions of Croatian wellness retreats, Dubrovnik serves as the perfect base for your explorations. The surrounding region offers an endless array of stunning landscapes and cultural encounters that will enrich your travel encounter, making each excursion from the city a new chapter in your discovery of Croatia.

Lokrum Island – A Tranquil Escape

Just a short boat ride from Dubrovnik lies Lokrum Island, a serene natural oasis and the perfect escape from the hustle and bustle of the city. This small, uninhabited island offers a mix of botanical gardens, ancient ruins, and hidden swimming spots, making it a favorite retreat for both locals and visitors.

What to Expect

Explore the lush greenery of the island's botanical gardens, where you'll find a wide variety of Mediterranean plants, cacti, and peacocks roaming freely. History lovers will appreciate the ruins of a 12th-century Benedictine monastery, while exploration seekers can hike up to Fort Royal, a Napoleonic fortress that offers panoramic views of Dubrovnik and the surrounding islands. Don't miss the chance to swim in the island's crystal-clear waters or float in the famous Dead Sea, a saltwater lake located in the heart of Lokrum.

How to Get There

Lokrum is just 15 minutes by boat from Dubrovnik's Old Town harbor. Boats run frequently throughout the day, making it an easy and convenient day trip.

Top Tip

Be sure to pack a picnic and enjoy lunch by the sea, as Lokrum has limited dining options. The island is a nature reserve, so there are no overnight stays—plan to return to Dubrovnik by sunset.

Day Trip to Korčula – Croatia's Island Gem

Known as the birthplace of Marco Polo, the island of Korčula is a stunning blend of history, culture, and natural beauty. This Adriatic jewel, with its medieval charm and pristine beaches, offers a perfect day trip from Dubrovnik for those looking to explore Croatia's rich maritime heritage.

What to See

• **Korčula Old Town**: Wander through the narrow, stone-paved streets of Korčula's Old Town, often referred to as "Little Dubrovnik" for its medieval fortifications and Venetian-style architecture. Visit St. Mark's Cathedral, a Gothic-Renaissance masterpiece, and explore the supposed house of Marco Polo, now a museum dedicated to the famous explorer.
• **Lumbarda**: Just outside the Old Town lies Lumbarda, a village known for its beautiful sandy beaches and vineyards. Sample some of the island's famous Grk wine, a local white varietal that is only produced in this region.
• **Beach Time**: Korčula boasts some of the most beautiful beaches in the Adriatic. Whether you prefer pebbled shores or secluded coves, the island offers plenty of spots to relax by the crystal-clear waters.

How to Get There

Ferries from Dubrovnik to Korčula operate regularly, with a travel time of about two hours. Private boat tours are also available for a more personalized encounter.

Top Tip

Try the local seafood—Korčula is known for its fresh catch of the day, including octopus, grilled fish, and scampi, all served with olive oil and locally grown herbs.

Ston and the Great Walls

Just an hour's drive from Dubrovnik, the town of Ston is famous for its impressive medieval walls and centuries-old salt pans. Ston's walls are often called the "European Wall of China" and are the longest fortifications in Europe, providing spectacular views of the Pelješac Peninsula.

What to Expect

Walk along the ancient walls that once protected this vital salt-producing town. The 5.5-kilometer-long fortifications connect the towns of Ston and Mali Ston, winding through hills and offering breathtaking views of the Adriatic Sea. Ston's salt pans, which have been in operation since Roman times, are still used to produce sea salt today—be sure to visit the salt pans and learn about the ancient methods of salt production.

How to Get There

Ston is located about 50 kilometers from Dubrovnik, easily accessible by car or bus.

Top Tip

Don't leave without trying the local oysters! Mali Ston is known for having some of the best oysters in the Adriatic, and many seaside restaurants offer fresh, delicious seafood.

Montenegro and the Bay of Kotor

For a trip past Croatia's borders, a day trip to Montenegro is a must. Just a short drive from Dubrovnik, the Bay of Kotor offers one of the most scenic and dramatic landscapes in the Balkans, with steep mountains plunging into the deep, blue waters of the Adriatic.

What to See

- **Kotor Old Town**: Explore the UNESCO-listed Old Town of Kotor, a maze of narrow streets, medieval churches, and charming squares. The town is surrounded by impressive city walls, and a hike up to the fortress of St. John offers incredible views of the bay.
- **Perast**: This picturesque village is famous for its two small islands, Our Lady of the Rocks and St. George. A boat trip to Our Lady of the Rocks is a must to visit the church and museum on this artificial island, built by sailors over centuries.
- **Budva**: For those interested in Montenegro's beach scene, Budva offers a mix of lively nightlife, historic Old Town charm, and some of the best beaches on the Adriatic.

How to Get There

Montenegro is about two hours by car from Dubrovnik. Guided tours are a popular way to explore Kotor and the surrounding area, with many tours offering hotel pick-up and drop-off services.

Top Tip

Bring your passport, as you'll be crossing an international border. Also, be prepared for the winding mountain roads—Montenegro's stunning landscapes are best appreciated with a steady hand on the wheel!

Mljet National Park – Croatia's Green Paradise

If you're looking for an island escape with unspoiled nature, head to Mljet National Park, located on the island of Mljet, one of the greenest and most pristine islands in Croatia.

What to Expect

Explore Mljet's famous saltwater lakes, Veliko and Malo Jezero, which are surrounded by pine forests and connected to the sea by a narrow channel. A small island in the middle of Veliko Jezero is home to a 12th-century Benedictine monastery, which you can visit by boat. The park also offers fantastic hiking and biking trails, allowing visitors to explore the island's lush landscapes and secluded coves.

How to Get There

Ferries from Dubrovnik to Mljet operate during the summer months, with a travel time of about an hour and a half.

Top Tip

Pack a picnic and enjoy a day of hiking, swimming, and exploring the natural beauty of Mljet's untouched wilderness.

Whether you're exploring hidden islands, walking the ancient walls of medieval towns, or crossing borders to uncover new cultures, Dubrovnik offers an incredible base for discovering the treasures of southern Croatia and past. So, grab your sunglasses, lace up your hiking boots, and set out on an unforgettable trip past the city walls—an exploration into the heart of the Adriatic awaits!

CHAPTER 10
Nightlife and Entertainment in Dubrovnik

Ah, Dubrovnik—where the sun sets over the sparkling Adriatic, casting a golden glow on ancient stone walls and narrow alleyways. By day, Dubrovnik amaze with its timeless beauty and rich history, but as night falls, the city transforms into a dynamic hub of culture, music, and entertainment. From classical performances in centuries-old venues to laid-back cocktail bars and lively beachside lounges, Dubrovnik's nightlife is as dynamic and enchanting as its sunlit streets. Whether you're seeking a quiet evening with a glass of wine overlooking the sea or an energetic night of music and dancing, Dubrovnik offers something for everyone. As you explore its bustling squares, charming courtyards, and hidden gems, you'll find that this coastal jewel has just as much magic after dark as it does under the Mediterranean sun.

Classical Music and Elegant Performances

For those who appreciate the finer things in life, Dubrovnik's cultural heritage shines brightest in its classical music concerts and elegant performances, often held in breathtaking historical settings that add an extra layer of enchantment to the evening.

Dubrovnik Summer Festival

The Dubrovnik Summer Festival is a highlight of the city's cultural calendar. Held every July and August, this prestigious event transforms Dubrovnik's stunning squares, fortresses, and palaces into open-air stages for world-class performances. From orchestral concerts to ballet and theater, the festival brings together artists from around the globe, offering a magical fusion of history and culture under the stars. Envision watching an opera in the courtyard of the Rector's Palace or enjoying a classical concert within the mighty walls of Fort Lovrijenac.

Rector's Palace Concerts

The Rector's Palace, a marvel of Gothic and Renaissance architecture, serves as one of Dubrovnik's most atmospheric venues for classical music performances. The intimate courtyard, with its grand arches and stone columns, creates a distinctive setting for chamber music and symphony concerts. Whether you're a seasoned fan of classical music or simply looking for a special evening out, a concert in this historic palace will leave you spellbound.

Sponza Palace and Sacred Music

For a truly spiritual encounter, the stunning Sponza Palace often hosts sacred music concerts, offering a serene and moving way to encounter Dubrovnik's rich cultural embroidery. The combination of soaring choral music with the palace's beautiful, acoustically resonant space provides an unforgettable evening for lovers of both history and music.

Beach Bars, Lounges, and Seaside Vibes

As the night unfolds in Dubrovnik, the city's beach bars and lounges come to life, offering a laid-back yet sophisticated atmosphere where you can sip cocktails and watch the waves gently lap against the shore.

Banje Beach Club

For those seeking a touch of luxury, Banje Beach Club, located just steps from the Old Town, offers a glamorous seaside encounter. By day, it's one of Dubrovnik's most popular beaches, but as the sun sets, it transforms into a chic lounge where you can sip on expertly crafted cocktails while enjoying breathtaking views of the Adriatic and the illuminated city walls. DJs spin smooth tunes as you relax on plush lounge chairs, making it the perfect spot for a stylish evening by the sea.

Buža Bar

Perched on the cliffs just outside Dubrovnik's city walls, Buža Bar is a must-visit for anyone looking to encounter the more relaxed, bohemian side of the city's nightlife. The bar's name translates to "hole-in-the-wall," and that's exactly what you'll find—a hidden entrance leading to a series of terraces carved into the rocks, offering unbeatable views of the sea. With a glass of local wine in hand, this is the ideal spot to unwind after a day of sightseeing, watching the sunset turn the horizon golden.

Sunset Lounge at Hotel Dubrovnik Palace

If you're in the mood for a more upscale encounter, head to the Sunset Lounge at Hotel Dubrovnik Palace. Overlooking the islands and coastline, this elegant bar offers an extensive cocktail menu and a luxurious setting, making it the perfect place to relax and enjoy the views as the day fades into night.

Trendy Bars and Nightlife Hotspots

For those who crave a more energetic nightlife scene, Dubrovnik offers a mix of trendy bars, dynamic nightclubs, and late-night venues where the music is always lively, and the drinks flow freely.

Revelin Club

Housed in a 16th-century fortress, Revelin Club is one of the most popular nightlife destinations in Dubrovnik. As one of Croatia's top electronic music venues, it regularly hosts international DJs and offers an incredible clubbing encounter within its massive stone walls. Whether you're a fan of techno, house, or dance music, Revelin is the place to dance the night away in Dubrovnik's Old Town.

Culture Club Revelin

Located within the fortress of Revelin, this high-energy nightclub is renowned for its stunning setting, with ancient stone walls creating a dramatic backdrop for its dynamic music scene. The club regularly hosts top international DJs and themed events, making it the perfect spot for those seeking an unforgettable night out in Dubrovnik.

D'Vino Wine Bar

For a more relaxed yet trendy evening, head to D'Vino Wine Bar, located in one of Dubrovnik's picturesque alleys. Specializing in local Croatian wines, this cozy spot is perfect for wine enthusiasts looking to explore the rich flavors of the region. The knowledgeable staff will guide you through a tasting of some of Croatia's finest varietals, from crisp whites to bold reds, making it a great start to an evening out.

Late-Night Cafes and Cocktails

Dubrovnik's café culture continues well into the night, with many places offering a laid-back atmosphere where you can sip coffee or cocktails and soak in the ambiance.

Art Café

Located near the city walls, Art Café is known for its eclectic décor, featuring colorful murals, quirky furnishings, and a relaxed vibe. This artsy spot is popular with both locals and tourists, offering everything from espresso to creative cocktails. It's a great place to unwind after a long day of exploring, or to kick off an evening out with friends.

Cave Bar More

For a truly distinctive encounter, visit Cave Bar More, located beneath Hotel More. This bar is set inside a natural cave, with tables located among the rock formations. The atmosphere is cool and intimate, offering a selection of signature cocktails and fine wines. It's an unforgettable place to enjoy a drink while marveling at the bar's distinctive setting.

Seasonal Events and Night Markets

Throughout the year, Dubrovnik hosts a variety of seasonal events and festivals that make the city's nightlife even more dynamic.

Dubrovnik Winter Festival

In the winter months, the Dubrovnik Winter Festival transforms the city into a wonderland of lights, music, and festive stalls. From Christmas markets in the Old Town to ice skating rinks and outdoor concerts, the festival brings a warm, joyful atmosphere to the city's streets. As night falls, the twinkling lights and holiday cheer create a magical backdrop for an evening of exploration.

Libertas Film Festival

Each summer, the Libertas Film Festival brings a touch of glamour to Dubrovnik, with outdoor screenings, red carpets, and celebrity appearances. The festival showcases films from around the world, turning Dubrovnik into a cinematic hub for several days. It's the perfect way to combine culture and nightlife, with many screenings and events happening under the stars.

CHAPTER 11
Practical Information for Travelers to Dubrovnik

Dubrovnik—a city where medieval fortresses meet the azure waters of the Adriatic, and cobblestone streets invite you to uncover centuries of history at every turn. As you plan your visit to this enchanting destination, it's important to be well-prepared with practical knowledge to ensure a smooth and memorable trip. From handling local currency and understanding health services to exploring accessible travel and embracing eco-friendly practices, this guide offers essential insights for a hassle-free stay in Dubrovnik.

Currency and Exchange Tips

Croatia uses the Croatian kuna (HRK) as its official currency. Dubrovnik, a popular destination for travelers, offers a variety of options for exchanging money and handling financial transactions. Knowing the best practices for managing currency can save you both time and money during your trip.

Using the Croatian Kuna (HRK)

The kuna comes in banknotes of 10, 20, 50, 100, and 200 HRK, while coins range from 1 to 5 kuna, along with smaller denominations in lipa (lp). Most businesses in Dubrovnik, including hotels, restaurants, and shops, accept major credit and debit cards, with contactless payments like Apple Pay and Google Pay widely available. However, it's always a good idea to carry some cash for smaller vendors and local markets, where cash may be preferred.

Currency Exchange

You'll find plenty of currency exchange offices (mjenjačnica) around Dubrovnik, especially in the Old Town and near major tourist areas. These usually offer competitive rates, but it's worth checking around for the best deals. While ATMs are also readily available, be mindful of any foreign transaction fees your bank may impose.

- **Top Tip**: Avoid exchanging money at airports or tourist hotspots like the city gates, as rates tend to be less favorable. Stick to reputable exchange offices in the city for better rates.

ATMs and Card Use

ATMs are widespread throughout Dubrovnik, and they accept most international cards, including Visa and Mastercard. It's a good idea to inform your bank of your travel plans before arriving to avoid any issues with card transactions. When withdrawing cash, always choose to be charged in the local currency (HRK) to get the best exchange rate.

- **Top Tip**: Be cautious of ATMs that offer dynamic currency conversion, as this usually results in higher fees. Always opt for being charged in kuna to avoid unfavorable exchange rates.

Emergency Contacts and Health Services

While Dubrovnik is a safe city with excellent healthcare, it's important to know what to do in case of an emergency. Croatia's healthcare system is modern and well-regarded, ensuring that medical help is always nearby if needed.

Emergency Numbers

- **112**: The EU-wide emergency number for police, fire, and ambulance services. Operators typically speak Croatian and English, making it easy to get help quickly.
- **194**: Direct number for medical emergencies.
- **192**: For police services.

Hospitals and Clinics

Dubrovnik General Hospital (Opća bolnica Dubrovnik) is the main hospital, well-equipped to handle emergencies and general healthcare needs. There are also several private clinics throughout the city that cater to tourists, offering English-speaking services. Pharmacies (ljekarna) are common and usually stock a wide range of over-the-counter medications.

- **Top Tip**: If you have travel insurance, ensure that your policy covers medical expenses in Croatia. EU citizens can use their European Health Insurance Card (EHIC) for medical treatment, but it's always wise to have additional coverage.

Accessibility in Dubrovnik

Dubrovnik, with its ancient walls and steep, narrow streets, can present challenges for travelers with disabilities, but the city has made strides in improving accessibility, particularly around major attractions and transport hubs.

Accessible Public Transport

Dubrovnik's buses are increasingly equipped with low-floor vehicles, allowing easier access for wheelchair users. While the Old Town's cobblestone streets can be tricky, many tourist attractions are making efforts to become more accessible, including ramps and guided assistance.

- **Top Tip**: Dubrovnik's Tourist Information Centers provide maps and advice for navigating the city's accessible routes.

Accessible Attractions

Landmarks like the Rector's Palace and the Dubrovnik Maritime Museum offer wheelchair access, while the city walls provide accessible viewing points. The cable car to Mount Srđ, a popular tourist attraction, is fully accessible, offering panoramic views of the city and the surrounding coast.

Traveling with Children

Dubrovnik is a family-friendly destination with plenty to offer for travelers with kids. From exploring the ancient city walls to enjoying boat trips around the islands, there's no shortage of activities to keep children entertained.

Family-Friendly Attractions

- **Lokrum Island**: A short boat ride from Dubrovnik, Lokrum offers beautiful beaches, botanical gardens, and roaming peacocks, making it a hit with kids.
- **Dubrovnik Aquarium**: Located within the Old Town, the aquarium is a fun and educational stop for families.
- **Sveti Jakov Beach**: A quieter alternative to the busier beaches, Sveti Jakov offers calm waters, perfect for swimming and beach games with children.

Child-Friendly Dining

Many restaurants in Dubrovnik cater to families, offering high chairs and children's menus. Look for casual dining spots along the waterfront or in the Old Town, where kids can sample local dishes like grilled fish or pasta while enjoying the lively atmosphere.

Sustainable Travel Tips

As one of Croatia's most popular tourist destinations, Dubrovnik is committed to preserving its natural and cultural heritage, making it a great place for eco-conscious travelers.

Public Transport and Walking

Dubrovnik is a compact city, perfect for exploring on foot. For longer distances, the city's efficient bus network runs on eco-friendly standards. Electric boats are also available for trips to nearby islands, reducing the environmental impact of your travels.

- **Top Tip**: Consider walking tours or cycling tours to explore the city and its surroundings while minimizing your carbon footprint.

Eco-Friendly Accommodation

Several hotels in Dubrovnik prioritize sustainability, with energy-efficient facilities, recycling programs, and water conservation efforts. Look for hotels with eco-certifications like Green Key, which ensures a commitment to environmentally friendly practices.

Reducing Waste

Dubrovnik encourages sustainable practices, with recycling bins placed throughout the city and many cafes and restaurants offering compostable packaging. Tap water is safe to drink, so bring a reusable bottle to reduce plastic waste during your stay.

Useful Apps and Resources for Tourists

To make your trip easier and more enjoyable, here are some must-have apps and resources that can help you guide through Dubrovnik like a local.

Dubrovnik Card App

The Dubrovnik Card App offers information on attractions, maps, and discounts for popular tourist spots. It's a great resource to have on hand as you explore the city.

Transport Apps: Moovit and Bolt

Moovit provides real-time information on Dubrovnik's public transport system, helping you find the quickest routes. Bolt is the preferred app for hailing affordable taxis or electric scooters, making short trips around the city a breeze.

Google Maps and Offline Guides

Google Maps is invaluable for navigating Dubrovnik's winding streets and finding your way to hidden gems. Download maps offline to ensure you always have access, even without mobile data.

By preparing yourself with these practical tips and insights, your trip to Dubrovnik will be both smooth and enriching. Whether you're exchanging currency, finding the best healthcare, or enjoying sustainable travel practices, this guide will help you make the most of your stay in this stunning coastal city. Get ready to uncover Dubrovnik's rich history, dynamic culture, and breathtaking beauty with confidence and ease.

CONCLUSION

As your trip through Dubrovnik draws to a close, the memories of its sun-soaked streets, breathtaking Adriatic views, and centuries-old fortifications will linger long after you leave. Dubrovnik, with its perfectly preserved medieval architecture and shimmering coastline, offers more than just a trip—it provides a window into a rich cultural embroidery where the past and present coalesce. Whether you've explored its iconic city walls, lost yourself in the winding streets of the Old Town, or ventured to the serene islands of the Elaphite Archipelago, Dubrovnik's timeless beauty and enduring spirit have surely left an indelible mark.

But Dubrovnik is more than a single encounter; it is a living city, one that invites you to delve deeper with each visit. It is a place where the rhythm of life moves with the ebb and flow of the Adriatic, where the culinary traditions speak of the sea and the land, and where festivals, art, and music fill the air with a constant sense of celebration. Past its postcard-perfect facade lies a community proud of its heritage, yet continuously developing, welcoming travelers to share in its dynamic story.

As you leave Dubrovnik, take with you not only the photographs but the essence of the city: the warmth of its people, the taste of its seafood, and the glow of its sunsets that seem to stretch endlessly over the sea. Dubrovnik is not a place you visit just once—it's a destination that calls you back, inviting you to uncover new layers of its charm each time. So, whether you return to climb its ancient walls once more, explore its lesser-known nooks, or simply bask in its serenity, Dubrovnik will always be there, waiting, its heart open to welcome you again.

Language and Communication

Basic Greetings and Introductions:

1. Bok – Hello
2. Dobro jutro – Good morning
3. Dobar dan – Good day
4. Dobra večer – Good evening
5. Laku noć – Good night
6. Kako si? – How are you?
7. Dobro, hvala – I'm fine, thank you
8. A ti? – And you?
9. Kako se zoveš? – What's your name?
10. Zovem se… – My name is…
11. Drago mi je – Nice to meet you
12. Bok – Bye
13. Doviđenja – Goodbye
14. Vidimo se kasnije – See you later
15. Vidimo se sutra – See you tomorrow

Polite Phrases:

1. Molim – Please
2. Hvala – Thank you

3. Puno hvala – Many thanks
4. Nema problema – No problem
5. Oprostite – Excuse me
6. Žao mi je – I'm sorry
7. Nema na čemu – You're welcome
8. Možete li mi pomoći? – Can you help me?
9. Govorite li engleski? – Do you speak English?
10. Ne razumijem – I don't understand
11. Možete li ponoviti? – Can you repeat that?
12. Sporije, molim – Slower, please
13. Koliko to košta? – How much does that cost?

Directions:

1. Gdje je...? – Where is...?
2. Gdje je WC? – Where is the bathroom?
3. Kako doći do željezničkog kolodvora? – How do I get to the train station?
4. Lijevo – Left
5. Desno – Right
6. Ravno – Straight ahead
7. Blizu – Nearby
8. Izgubio sam se – I am lost
9. Možete li mi pokazati put? – Can you show me the way?

At the Hotel:

1. Imam rezervaciju – I have a reservation
2. Imate li slobodnu sobu? – Do you have a free room?
3. Koliko košta noćenje? – How much is one night?

4. Mogu li se prijaviti? – Can I check in?
5. Gdje je lift? – Where is the elevator?
6. Koja je lozinka za Wi-Fi? – What is the Wi-Fi password?
7. Možete li naručiti taksi za mene? – Can you call me a taxi?
8. Kada je doručak? – When is breakfast?
9. Ima li restorana u blizini? – Is there a restaurant nearby?

At the Restaurant:

1. Želim... – I would like...
2. Što preporučujete? – What do you recommend?
3. Ima li jelovnik na engleskom? – Is there a menu in English?
4. Je li ovo vegetarijansko? – Is this vegetarian?
5. Alergičan sam na... – I'm allergic to...
6. Vodu, molim – A water, please
7. Bilo je ukusno – That was delicious
8. Mogu li dobiti račun? – Could I have the bill?
9. Napojnica – Tip
10. Mogu li platiti karticom? – Can I pay by card?

Shopping:

1. Imate li ovo u mojoj veličini? – Do you have this in my size?
2. Samo gledam – I'm just looking
3. To je previše skupo – That's too expensive
4. Mogu li to probati? – Can I try this on?

5. Ima li popusta? – Is there a discount?
6. Želim ovo kupiti – I want to buy this
7. Imate li vrećicu? – Do you have a bag?
8. Možete li ovo zapakirati? – Can you wrap it?

Transportation:

1. Jedna karta za... – A ticket to...
2. Kada polazi vlak? – When does the train leave?
3. Gdje je autobusni kolodvor? – Where is the bus station?
4. Koliko košta karta? – How much is a ticket?
5. Želim iznajmiti bicikl – I would like to rent a bike
6. Kako doći do podzemne željeznice? – How do I get to the subway?
7. Ide li ovaj vlak za...? – Does this train go to...?
8. Koliko traje putovanje? – How long is the trip?

Sightseeing:

1. Možete li preporučiti muzej? – Can you recommend a museum?
2. Gdje je najbliži turistički ured? – Where is the nearest tourist office?
3. Ima li ovdje vođena tura? – Is there a guided tour here?

4. Koje su turističke atrakcije ovdje? – What are the tourist attractions?

5. Mogu li slikati? – Can I take photos?

6. Koliko košta ulaznica? – How much is the entrance fee?

7. Vrijeme i datumi: Time and Dates

8. Koliko je sati? – What time is it?

9. Danas – Today

10. Sutra – Tomorrow

11. Prekosutra – The day after tomorrow

12. Jučer – Yesterday

13. U koliko sati? – At what time?

14. Koliko traje? – How long does it take?

Numbers (1-10):

1. Jedan – One
2. Dva – Two
3. Tri – Three
4. Četiri – Four
5. Pet – Five
6. Šest – Six

7. **Sedam – Seven**
8. **Osam – Eight**
9. **Devet – Nine**
10. **Deset – Ten**

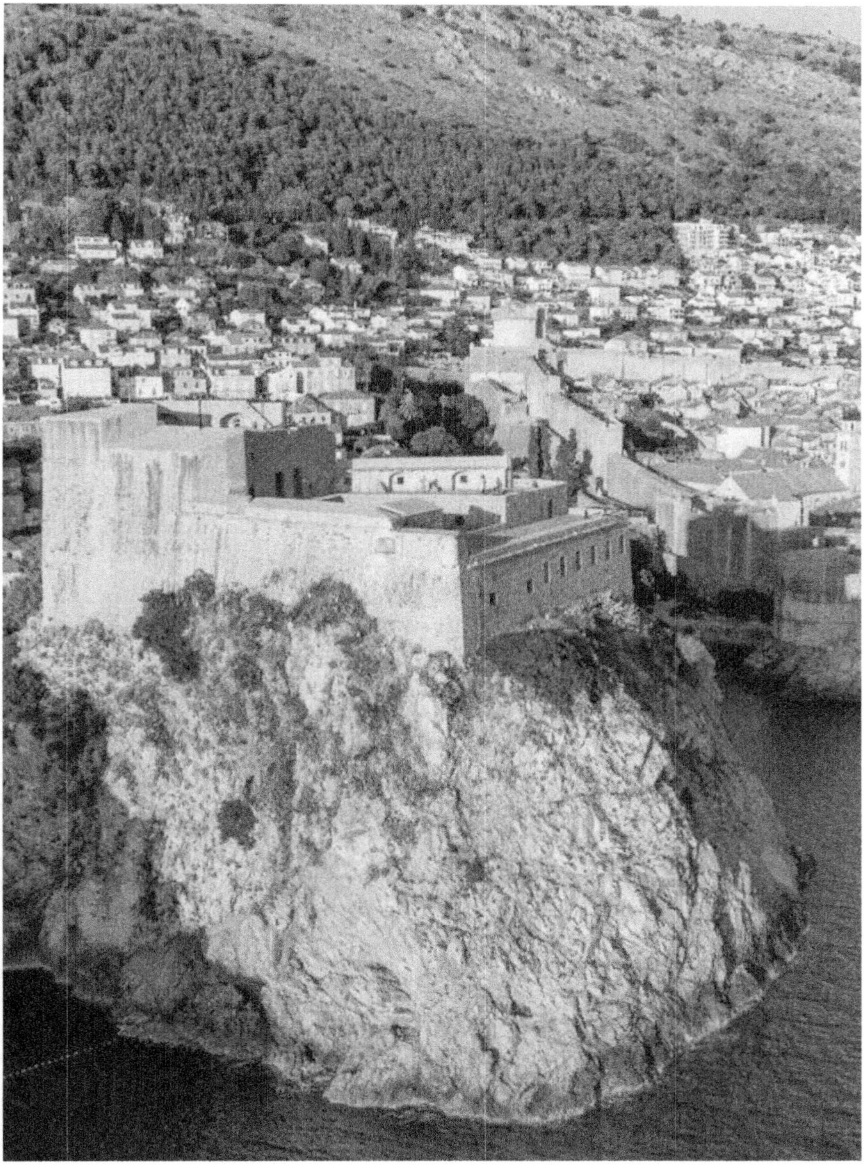

THANK YOU

Thank you for joining me on this journey through my book. I hope it has brought you as much joy to read as it did for me to create. Your feedback means a great deal, and I'd love to hear your thoughts on your experience.

If this story has sparked your imagination, offered new perspectives, or simply added to your reading enjoyment, I kindly invite you to share a review on Amazon. Your words have the power to guide others and play a crucial role in helping my book reach more readers.

An honest review not only provides insight for future readers but also helps increase my book's visibility in the vast world of literature. Every review is deeply appreciated and truly makes a difference.

Thank you so much for taking the time to share your thoughts. Your support means everything to me, and I look forward to hearing how the story has touched you

Printed in Great Britain
by Amazon